Making Your
Husband *feel* Loved

Compiled by Betty Malz

Making Your Husband *feel* Loved

20 Christian Women
Share Their Secrets for a
Fresh & Exciting Marriage

Compiled by Betty Malz

CREATION
HOUSE
Orlando, FL

MAKING YOUR HUSBAND FEEL LOVED by Betty Malz
Published by Creation House
Strang Communications Company
600 Rinehart Road
Lake Mary, Florida 32746
Web site http://www.creationhouse.com

Unless otherwise noted, all Scripture quotations are from the New American Standard Bible. Copyright © 1960, 1962, 1963, 1968, 1971, 1972, 1973, 1975, 1977 by the Lockman Foundation. Used by permission.

Scripture quotations marked KJV are from the King James Version of the Bible.

Scripture quotations marked RSV are from the Revised Standard Version of the Bible. Copyright © 1946, 1952, 1971 by the Division of Christian Education of the National Council of the Churches of Christ in the USA. Used by permission.

Scripture quotations marked NKJV are from the New King James Version of the Bible. Copyright © 1979, 1980, 1982 by Thomas Nelson Inc., publishers. Used by permission.

Scripture quotations marked AMP are from the Amplified Bible. Old Testament copyright © 1965, 1987 by the Zondervan Corporation. The Amplified New Testament copyright © 1954, 1958, 1987 by the Lockman Foundation. Used by permission.

Scripture quotations marked NIV are from the Holy Bible, New International Version. Copyright © 1973, 1978, 1984, International Bible Society. Used by permission.

Scripture quotations marked TLB are from the The Living Bible, copyright © 1971. Used by permission of Tyndale House Publishers, Inc., Wheaton, Illinois 60189. All right reserved.

Library of Congress Cataloging-in-Publication Data:
MAKING YOUR HUSBAND FEEL LOVED : 20 CHRISTIAN WOMEN SHARE THEIR
    SECRETS FOR A FRESH & EXCITING MARRIAGE / compiled by Betty Malz.
            p.   cm.
        ISBN: 0–88419–534–1 (pbk.)
        1. Marriage—Religious aspects—Christianity. 2. Wives—Religious
life. 3. Wives—Conduct of life. I. Malz, Betty.
BV835.M225 1998   97-48824
248.8'435—dc21   CIP

Printed in the United States of America
89012345 BBG 87654321

Contents

Contents

Introduction

by Betty Malz

Every human being has two basic needs: *To love and to be loved*. Many books have been written on the marriage relationship. This book answers one question: "How do I make my husband feel really loved?"

Men: Do yourself a favor. Buy this book for your fianceé before she becomes your wife. Or, if you're already married, mail it anonymously to your wife.

Women: This is not a manual on how to become a smiling doormat or how to eat humble pie gracefully while *he* dines on cake and ice cream. Leo F. Buscaglia says, "Even though you are only half of a relationship, you must remain a whole person, apart from the relationship. Value yourself, too. The only people who appreciate a doormat are people with dirty shoes."*

Carl and I have conducted marriage seminars where I spoke to the men and let them speak back to me. He has talked to the women and listened to their complaints and needs. In this book I use some practical illustrations gleaned from these informal surveys.

All of the writers in this book speak from experience, including me. When I said "I do" to Carl Malz, my second husband, I became a bride, wife, pastor's wife, second wife, mother, stepmother, grandmother, and mother-in-law.

Shortly after we did our first marriage seminar together we sat down and made a list of the many ways in which we are opposite. It totaled thirty-four. We laughingly tell people, "We have been married four wonderful years—eighteen altogether!" If we can make it, you can too.

I feel sorry for men. They work all week in a box called a factory or office, eat a boxed lunch, ride in a box called a car, sit two hours on Sunday in a box called a church, stop for a quick bite in a box called a restaurant, watch a box called television, fall into a box called a bed—and start all over again. When they are tired and old we put them in a box called a casket. No wonder that when a man hits fifty he feels all boxed in!

Many men feel cheated that they must first sell their lives and energy for several decades to make a living for wives who snag them with sex appeal

---

*From *Loving Each Other,* Slack, 1984

then play the game of "bait and switch" after marriage. Love needs a revival!

I have found five things essential for a man to feel loved and for a marriage to survive: health, sense of humor, prayer, other relationships, and frequent renewal.

Health: Ladies, take care of your health. God works healing miracles, but happiness is home-made. Do your homework. Eat light, lose weight if necessary, drink lots of water, and get enough sleep and exercise. Take care of yourself. You can be replaced.

I was telling this to a couple recently. The woman leaned over to her husband and asked, "Honey, if I die, are you going to get married again?"

He replied, "Probably. You know I hate going to funerals alone." Which brings me to the next essential ingredient for a successful marriage.

Sense of humor: Laugh together. Look for things during the day to laugh with him about at the dinner table. Cut out clippings to share or to mail to him at work. One doctor has said that a person who laughs a lot and smiles frequently will have a happy marriage and, after forty, will look seven-and-a-half years younger than his or her age.

I have taken the same survey with twenty-year-olds and with people facing retirement: "If you were looking for a mate, number the following 1 through 7 according to importance: size, age, education, looks, religion, sense of humor, and money." Over 80 percent stated that a sense of humor was number one in importance.

Be creative. When there is no money, use your imagination. Once Carl and I could not go out to eat, so we waded a creek to a big rock midstream and sat in the sun enjoying a sack lunch. Another time when the house was full of company we took intimate sanctuary in the hayloft of our barn above the horse stable, laughed at our cunning, and made love.

Prayer: My husband is as smart as a tree full of owls. I majored in kids and minored in quarter-horses. I have always felt he was spiritually superior, so I never prayed for him. Recently I started praying for him early each morning. I am surprised at how much better a man he is becoming! You cannot stay mad at anyone you are praying for.

Don't let the sun go down on your wrath (Eph. 4:26). Initiate reconciliation, lovemaking, and forgiveness. It feels good to forgive, and there is a reward to the peacemaker. God won't hear my prayer if I don't forgive. He who refuses to forgive breaks the bridge he himself must cross to get to God.

Forgive—and then forget. Throw away the records. Refuse to look back on past quarrels and disappointments, but look ahead to hope.

Other relationships: Have fun times with other happy couples your age. This is a good thermometer for your own relationship. Don't hang around with people who don't like you, who make you feel uncomfortable. Even Jesus had to shake the dust off His feet in some places.

Frequent renewal: For years I drove an old 1962 MGA convertible. Even though old, it was a delight to drive or ride in. It got thirty-seven miles per gallon as long as I took it for regular tune-ups. In my marriage, I periodically need to tune up, check up, to see if I'm out of sync. There should be a sign on the highway of life: *Construction Zone for the Next Forty Years.* The road to success is always under construction. You have to work at making your marriage better. Build up your husband; compliment him; pray for him several times a day. All this pays big dividends. Your husband feels loved, and you feel loved! ♥

Betty Malz is a survivor. She was born to pioneer pastors at the end of the Great Depression. She survived four brothers, a ruptured appendix, throat surgery, spinal surgery, a tornado in Indiana, a hurricane in Florida, and being thrown from a fast-running horse. Her first husband died during open-heart surgery, leaving Betty pregnant with their second baby. With two little girls she survived for six years on Social Security and bouillon cubes. Then she met Carl Malz, who had survived a wife's death from cancer. When Betty said "I do" to him, she became a bride, wife, pastor's wife, mother, stepmother, grandmother, mother-in-law—and now her initials are B. M.! Her first book, *My Glimpse of Eternity* (Revell), has sold two million copies and has been translated into eighteen languages. Carl and Betty live in Crystal Beach, Florida. Carl teaches in foreign missions assignments for the Assemblies of God, which have included assignments in Russia, Peru, the Gamabia (West Africa), and India.

Part One

Let Your Love Show

Accept the Challenge

by Ingrid Trobisch

Sounds easy, doesn't it, to show your husband you really love him? However, two friends of mine, David and Vera Mace, liken the wedding day to two truckloads of raw material being dumped on an empty lot. Out of the mess and confusion the husband and wife have to build their marriage.

It's a lifelong challenge.

Showing our husbands we love them is part of that challenge. Actually, what's easy (at least for some) is saying the words "I love you." But to live those words is another matter. When you consider all the stresses of our everyday lives—the kids, the house, the job, finances, relationships—showing our husbands we love them each day can be a real labor of love. But most things worth doing are never easy.

We are off to a great start if we first admit to ourselves that we are imperfect people with imperfect marriages—and imperfect lives. To love indefinitely means to say, "I am sorry."

Going back to that empty lot, we need to learn to throw out our old garbage. I happen to love trash day. A couple of men come in a big truck and carry all the junk away so I can make a clean start. I've had to learn when it's time to throw out the old junk in our relationship—and to forget it when it's gone. It does us no good to be like the wife who buried the hatchet but left the handle sticking out. We can best show our husbands we love them by asking forgiveness when we're wrong and forgiving them when they're wrong.

Husbands are only human. They are not the rocks of Gibraltar they sometimes pretend to be or that we sometimes want them to be. When we accept these men as our husbands, we agree to a lifetime partnership. The key word here is "accept." Men need to be accepted for who they are, just as we do. Remember, we have a lifetime to share. Take a deep breath. Life is a process. Let's flow with it and not be in a hurry.

Basically, showing our husbands we love them requires nothing more than good common sense and discipline. According to my late husband, Walter, men need three basic things: *praise, food,* and *rest.*

Of the three, *praise* is most important. A woman often doesn't realize that behind her husband's valiant exterior can be a very fragile ego. Paul

Popence, the pioneer of American marriage counseling, reportedly said, "Men are hard but brittle. Women are soft but tough." The point is perhaps best made by a wise, elderly woman I know. When I asked her how a wife could really love her husband, she replied without hesitation, "Brag 'em up." In other words, tell them each day they are doing a good job—whether they are raking the leaves or helping in the kitchen. Complimenting someone else makes us feel better anyway. So what is there to lose?

The second basic is *food*. We all need food to survive. My advice: Make sure your husband can function at his best by feeding him properly and on time. He really will be less grumpy that way! Don't aggravate a situation—just feed him. Be a positive caregiver, especially if you are the one responsible for the preparation of daily meals. Of course, no one expects you to be a Julia Child, singing out of the kitchen with a platter of incredible delicacies every night. Just do it, and do it on time. Be sure the table is set fifteen minutes before you expect your husband to come home. It worked for Walter and me.

The last basic is *rest*. Give the poor guy a break. At one of our ministry's marriage seminars a man commented, "When I come home from work, I just want to snore awhile." Another added, "I'd like to be in a quiet room—where there's no wind, no storm brewing—when I've finished a hard day's work." Obviously he wasn't talking about the weather.

Of course, we've had a hard day's work, too, as homemakers, mothers, or working wives. I'm not saying it's easy. But we need to make the effort if our goal is to show our husbands we love them.

3

Take the signs seriously. Don't pressure him when he's tired or feeling down. Be an energizer, a strength-giver, for your husband. Allow him his own place—his corner or easy chair or desk—where it's off-limits to disturb him. "Let there be spaces in your togetherness," the poet Kahlil Gibran once wrote. Besides, if we learn to give each other space, the time will be much more rewarding when we come together again.

It's been said, "Life would not be so hard if we did not expect it to be so easy." We Americans are spoiled. We have much more than we need, yet it seems we are never satisfied. Many young people grow up believing they will get everything they want. They also believe it should happen quickly without any hard work on their part. Instant gratification. But life is not easy. Neither is marriage. It takes hard work. However, if we take one day at a time and add to each day a little love, patience, understanding, discipline, and humor, all our hard work will pay off.

I know.

Forty years ago I was preparing to leave the States to become a missionary in Cameroon, West Africa. A young German exchange student whom I barely knew attended my commissioning service in Rock Island, Illinois. Recently I read for the first time what he wrote in his journal the following day, January 24, 1949: "Yesterday I cleaned up my room. Then I went to the commissioning service of Ingrid Hult. She is twenty-three years old, clear, committed, ready for any battle, and yet every inch a woman. Such a person I would marry without a moment's hesitation."

I was strangely comforted as I read those words, penned in a bold German script. Back then I didn't have a clue about his feelings. I left for France and Africa, and he and I were continents apart. But three years later we did get married. We had a lifetime of wonderful adventures together before God called Walter home in October 1979.

I have a feeling many husbands would echo Walter's wish for his wife: to be clear, committed, a helpmate ready for any challenge, and, at the same time, completely a woman.

It was not always easy for me. I made mistakes, and I failed at times. Remember, this was his description, not my own! But I know every effort I made to be these things for Walter—to show him I loved him—seemed to multiply exponentially over the years. Indeed you do reap what you sow.

Accept the challenge. Show your husband you love him. It's worth every effort you make. ♥

Ingrid Trobisch's education prepared her to be a missionary teacher in French-speaking Africa. A young pastor from Germany named Walter Trobisch shared her vision. In 1953, a year after they married, they left for Cameroon, West Africa. In 1965 they moved their family to a hamlet in the Austrian Alps where Walter and Ingrid continued their work as counselors, best-selling authors, lecturers, and finally as co-founders of the international Family Life Mission, bringing biblical messages on marriage and family life. In 1982, three years after Walter's death, Ingrid returned to the place of her childhood, the Ozark Mountains. Here she continues writing, lecturing, and enjoying her five children and thirteen grandchildren. Her latest book is titled *Keeper of the Springs* (Multnomah).

2

Little Things
Mean a Lot

by Sandra Simpson LeSourd

Sᴛᴏᴘ! Lᴏᴏᴋ! Lɪsᴛᴇɴ! Three commanding words. But three little words that when heeded will breathe new life into a humdrum, sagging marriage relationship. But how do we switch gears in our hectic lives to heed these warnings? And how do we change in relation to our husbands? Change can be a dirty word for most of us.

For the sincere seeker who is determined that life with her husband can be better, I say, "Take the plunge." The rewards of a rekindled marriage are certainly worth a little inconvenience, even some pain. Be fearless. Go for it!

Let's say it's Saturday morning and your husband

is feeling romantically inclined. You have been waiting for weeks for the "Year-end 75%-Off Sale" at your favorite dress shop—and that's just one of the stops on your long list of errands. You feel about as much like making love as scrubbing the bathroom.

"I'll be home by 4:30," you quickly promise. "When I get back, I'll slip into something comfortable. We'll take the phone off the hook and. . . . "

"But 4:30 is when the bowl game starts. I'm in the mood right now."

Having a root canal appointment is one thing. But if you're repotting your African violets or alphabetizing your spice rack or even planning a shopping trip, draw a deep breath and tell yourself *these things can wait.*

So *stop!* If you don't, the mood will be gone as far as he's concerned, and you may miss something spontaneous and lovely. Romance during half-time of the game won't be the same for him.

Being able to stop what you're doing (call it flexibility if you like) is sometimes difficult but necessary in enhancing your marriage.

Perhaps your husband comes home after work one day and says, "Let's drive out to the beach, watch the sunset, and grab a bite to eat." He's trying to be creative and spontaneous and suggest something special he feels will please you. Now this can be a problem with children at home, but arrangements can usually be made for child care. Flow with his adventurous spirit. Even if dinner has been planned or is already in the oven, it usually can be resurrected for a later meal.

My husband, Len, and I try to have a date night once a week. We realize how important time alone together is in this turbulent world. Sometimes our special date involves going out for a meal—breakfast dates are a favorite of ours—but it can be both creative and inexpensive. It can be as simple as a long walk and an ice cream cone. Or popcorn by the fire or candlelight where we take time for personal talk.

One husband I know had a unique idea for a yearly "second honeymoon" on their wedding anniversary. Since he and his wife were parents of eight, their lives at home were chaotic. They couldn't afford expensive trips, so he rented a lovely room at a local hotel for a long weekend. In three days this couple did all the things they didn't have time to do during the year: tennis, dinner and dancing, shopping, sleeping in late. They returned home refreshed and renewed after their "hometown vacation."

If we learn to stop we will certainly be ready to take the next step.

Look. To look may seem simple. We hear often of "removing the scales from our eyes." Do I really see my husband? During courtship I noticed every flicker of Len's deep blue eyes, every furtive sigh or posture change. But somewhere along the way my powers of observation have relaxed. I get busy with important family and home responsibilities. Sometimes when he arrives home I am on the telephone. He's in and out before I finish my call. Sometimes he tries to tell me something when the phone rings, and when I finish talking he's involved in a project of his own. Communication in our home is often broken and unfinished.

I'm learning to *look* at my husband when he

comes home. The secret here is to see him through his body language. How he walks, moves his head, uses his hands. Len doesn't talk about his down feelings easily. He'll present a relaxed "everything is fine" front at times when something in my spirit says he's upset. So I study him carefully. The tired look in his eyes may give it away, or the sag of his shoulders, or an edge of irritability in his voice. That's when I need to stop everything else, look at him directly and ask, "OK, what's gone wrong?" If he has my complete attention, he'll almost always open up.

Study your husband's body language. Sometimes we need to "hear" with our eyes. His body language often tells us more than he is saying. Know when he is down or hurting deeply about something. Know when to comfort him, and affirm him when he is feeling stressed. Your words of love and encouragement can soothe his wounds and breathe vitality into his bruised, sagging spirit. You are his safe harbor. His best friend. Look for ways to show him how much you care.

When Len is down and I have to leave for an appointment, I tuck an "I love you" note into his shirt pocket or in the toe of his tennis shoe. So often it's the little things that are special blessings to our spouses. When you're shopping, bring home the latest issue of his favorite magazine. Surprise him with iced tea when he's mowing the lawn.

Here's another way to *look*. Check out your husband to see if he needs some assistance in the fashion department. Many men are sadly lacking in sartorial skills—they often appear to have been dressed by a committee. Most men are grateful for help in this area. A few diehards may insist they look terrific when they've mixed two different plaids and a floral tie, but don't despair.

One of our daughters-in-law talked my husband into getting his "colors" done—an activity he disdained as being strictly feminine. But he emerged from the session triumphant. "I'm a winter!" he beamed. "I guess I'll have to concede I've got some clothes that aren't in my best colors."

"Hallelujah," I said under my breath.

A news story once told about Mikhail Gorbachev's wearing brown sport shoes with a navy pin-striped suit when he was in China. The Occidental Press was horrified. Didn't the Soviet leader take the meetings seriously?

I wondered if his wife, Raisa, was polishing his black dress shoes back in the Kremlin to be expressed to Taipai?

Few of us are dressing our husbands for summit meetings, but we can help them avoid the most glaring disasters—if they'll let us.

Stop, look, and, perhaps most important, *listen.*

I especially like to talk on the telephone. Could it be that I like the sound of my own voice too much? Let's face it—many of us women talk more than we listen. Yet something in the past five years has changed me.

When I married Len in June 1985, we began a tradition of starting each day by praying together for one hour. We intercede for all the members of both our families (fifty-three people). Every day we pray for them. We pray for special friends, associates, neighbors; we pray for pastors and local and world leaders.

We do something else too. We ask God for His word to us for the day, for His guidance and direction.

Then we listen. This is new for me. I haven't done much listening in my life. But I am learning to hear God's voice—and then obey it.

This has helped me listen to my husband as well. He has wisdom to give me as I learn to shut up and let him speak.

If my husband and I are driving in the car, listening to a tape, and he begins to talk, I shut off the tape to listen. Conversations between us are too valuable—I don't want to miss one word of them. This has also taught me to listen more to my friends.

Len kids me today by saying he used the "Stop . . . look . . . listen" technique with me right after we met. On our first date in August 1984 he *stopped* at my home for dessert and coffee. I showed him my fireside hearth, where I occasionally served myself communion.

When he *looked* startled, I asked him, "Do you think this is improper?"

"Not at all. I think it's a fine way to build a closer relationship with God," he replied.

"Would you have communion with me now?" I asked him.

He *listened* to my procedure, then we knelt at the altar, shared the communion elements and ended by praying together. A beautiful experience. From then on it was clear to us that God was in our courtship and had a special plan for us as a team.

I urge you not only to *stop, look, and listen* to your mate, but to find ways to adopt these three commanding words in your relationship with the

Lord. He'll give you His marching orders, put His love and healing into your life, and heap His blessings upon you, "pressed down, shaken together, and overflowing." ♥

Sandra Simpson LeSourd is the widow of Leonard LeSourd, who served as associate publisher of Chosen Books and president of Breakthrough, Inc. (a nonprofit prayer ministry). Sandy is a lecturer on chemical dependency and compulsive behavior. Sandy serves on the national board of directors for several groups, including Breakthrough, Inc., Christian Healing Ministries, the Christian TV and Film Commission, and on the international board of directors for Tapestry, a worldwide Christian women's prayer ministry. She has three grown children and one grandchild. She lives on Scarlet Oak Farm in Hillsboro, Virginia.

3

Loving Him His Way

by Evelyn Roberts

I THINK I BEGAN to love my husband the first time I met him, although it took two years for God to bring us together in marriage. I say God brought us together because without His intervention we never would have been married.

In the beginning I loved Oral because I knew God put us together and because I felt a physical attraction to him. He met my specifications of what I wanted in a husband.

In the years I have lived with him my love has grown to be much more. I have respect, admiration, appreciation, and compassion for him, and loyalty to him.

15

Love in the beginning of a marriage is one thing, and love after fifty years of being together is another.

That is not to say we have not had difficult times—we have. But I learned one thing early on. Husbands do not like to be nagged.

When we first married, Oral was not as tidy with his clothes as I thought he should be. He threw his dirty clothes on the floor. So I told him to put them in the hamper. He didn't. I kept harping at him every day until one day he looked at me. He didn't say a word—but that look said, "Evelyn, hush! I've had enough!"

I sat down and had a talk with myself: *Evelyn, how much is your marriage worth to you? You could be without a husband and never have to pick up dirty clothes, but is that what you want?* I never said another word to Oral, and soon he began to pick up his clothes and put them in the hamper. I think that day I learned that there are high values and low values, and I loved Oral so much I was willing to take whatever came with the package.

It is true I have catered to Oral in many ways. My children tell me I have spoiled him, and that's why he doesn't know much about providing food for himself or taking care of mundane things.

Now sometimes I wish I had insisted that he learn to fix his own meals. He is so helpless he doesn't even know how to make coffee. He can cook an egg but he burns the skillet. The children used to ask him to fix their bicycles, but he didn't know one thing about fixing bicycles or any other mechanical object.

However, Oral has catered to me, too. He has always treated me like a queen, especially when I was pregnant. I felt so big and awkward before my babies were born, and when Oral would ask me to go somewhere with him, I would always find excuses not to go out in public where people would see me. I remember once he said to me, "Evelyn, you are more beautiful than you've ever been. I'm proud you're my wife and you are carrying our baby. I would kiss you in the streets of Chicago and let the world know I love you." Now who wouldn't love and appreciate a man like that!

Our marriage has been special because both of us have worked at it. But at least one time I didn't work hard enough to see his real needs.

In the early days of our crusades I couldn't always go with him because of the children. So just before Oral came home, Rebecca, our oldest daughter, and I would sit down and plan the meals we would have when her dad came home. We knew what his favorite foods were so we made sure they were on the menu. A few evenings after his homecoming from one of these trips, Oral said to me, "Evelyn, put the children to bed. I want to talk to you." When the children were tucked in bed, I joined him in the den and closed the door.

He said, "Evelyn, there's something wrong with our marriage."

My eyebrows flew up. "There is?"

"Yes," he said. "You haven't paid any attention to me since I've been home. It's like I don't exist. You spend time with the children but none with me."

"Oral," I replied, not at all calmly, "I have spent hours fixing your favorite foods. I have asked the children to be on the best behavior and let you rest. I've tried so hard to please you. Honey, you are gone so much you don't know what a normal marriage is like."

He said, "I don't want a normal marriage. I want an above normal marriage—the best anyone has ever had!"

Well, as you can imagine, there was a lot of apologizing, kissing, hugging, and lovemaking that night, for I realized that, even though I hadn't know it before, he felt I was ignoring him.

Since then I have learned that no matter what I feel in my heart for my husband, unless I tell him and show him *in ways he can understand,* he really doesn't know I love him.

We have learned, when there is so much to do, just to sit down together, hold hands, and tell each other exactly how we feel. When bad times come, Oral knows I support him, and that makes the struggles so much easier.

So often we stand together and agree in prayer just before he leaves for a difficult business meeting or a potentially unpleasant encounter, and we feel God's presence standing with us. We know everything will turn out all right.

I married with never a thought of ever leaving my husband. It was a "till death do us part" ceremony. That attitude is stronger now than ever because I truly love him—strengths, faults, and all. Just the way he wants. ♥

Evelyn Roberts is wife of evangelist Oral Roberts and was his helpmate in founding Oral Roberts University. They have been married fifty-one years and have four children and thirteen grandchildren. Evelyn spends most of her time ministering to the needs of her husband and helping him answer letters from hurting people. She is the author of several books, including *His Darling Wife, Evelyn* and a children's book, *Heaven Has a Floor.*

4

Learn What to Expect From Your Relationship

by Cathy Lechner

ANYONE IN THE VALLEY? Isaiah tells us, "A voice of one calling: 'In the desert prepare the way for the Lord . . . Every valley shall be raised up'" (40:3–4, NIV).

Just cry out and say, "Lift me up, Lord." Every valley will be lifted up and every mountain and hill made low. Some of you have high highs and low lows. You don't know anything in between. Not every experience has to be a valley or a mountaintop. Sometimes it's just life. Not everything is either God or the devil. "The devil just blew out my tire, and it's flat. Oh, that devil." No! It was a nail that did it. It's just life; it's stuff; it just happens.

> And the crooked shall be made straight, and
> the rough places plain.
>
> —ISAIAH 40:4, KJV

Do you have a lot of rough places? Make them a plain.

> And the glory of the Lord shall be revealed,
> and all flesh shall see it together: for the
> mouth of the Lord hath spoken it.
>
> —ISAIAH 40:5, KJV

We are seeing the glory of the Lord today. There are some folks in Jacksonville who have meetings called "Fire and Glory." They just get together and sing, laugh, and cry. Can you remember the first time you were touched by God? You can't forget it. Do you long for that experience again? You don't want to go back in time, because you paid a big price to get where you are right now. But you want a renewal of that touch.

You have heard that God will never share His glory with another. That's scriptural. But you need to go back and research that scripture. We take it out of context and apply it to people we think are getting too big for their britches. God was referring to false and foreign gods. The apostle said that this was a mystery, "Christ in you, the hope of glory" (Col. 1:27, KJV). If He didn't want me to have this glory, why would Paul say that?

I'm a glory junkie. I'm a power junkie. I want the glory of God. I want the anointing of God. And however it manifests itself, I don't care, I want it. If I laugh, cry, pray, travail, sit quietly, or run around the church, I just want the glory of God. There is a glory that comes from on high to us individually, but there is a greater glory, a corporate glory, that comes when we are gathered in one place and God sovereignly comes and touches us and fills the room and stirs our spirits.

But there's another kind of glory. It's the glory that comes from within, the mystery glory. Christ in us, being released and revealed. I can go to a meeting, and if His anointing is there I can be stirred. But if I do not learn the greater glory, the mature glory of Christ *in* me, then I'm stirred but not changed. I want to be changed from glory to glory to glory. That's the glory that comes from within, not from without. It comes from going through trials, temptations, bitter circumstances, and attacks from the enemy and by continually saying, "But God's Word has said . . . "

Isaiah was in the temple the year that King Uzziah died. The Word says, "I saw also the Lord sitting upon a throne, high and lifted up, and his train [His glory] filled the temple" (Isa. 6:1, KJV). Isaiah wasn't alone in the temple. Others were there with him. But they were all busy mourning the death of King Uzziah. When the glory of the Lord was revealed only one man saw it—Isaiah.

You've got to look beyond the circumstances, death, pressure, and your trials. When God is lifted up, His glory fills the place. We are the temple of the Holy Ghost, and His glory can fill that temple as well.

Isaiah 60:1 tells us to arise. There is something about simply arising. You don't need to learn fifteen steps to an overcoming life. You just need to arise. Get up, and be sure you are standing up on the inside as well as on the outside.

Some things don't change even though you've walked with Jesus for many years. Some principles don't change, whether you are a veteran Christian or a new believer. Arise. Pull yourself up. Stand up. From what? From the depression that circumstances have put you in. Circumstances and resulting depression will keep you down.

To depress means to push upon something. You need to arise. The Bible doesn't say, "Bind the devil for four hours, or call sixteen intercessors and have them stand with you." Nor does it say, "Stay home from church and watch your favorite television pastor. Going is too hard, and today you don't want to be with happy people who are just a bunch of hypocrites anyway."

The Word tells us to *get up*. You're down there because circumstances have forced you down. But you don't have to stay there. Get up! Arise.

And shine. Be radiant, for your light has come and the glory of the Lord has risen upon you. The glory of the Lord will never come upon you if you don't get up. It will never be released in you if you will not arise. If you stay in your circumstances, you'll never see the glory of the Lord come. The glory of the Lord is on a higher plane.

"For behold, darkness shall cover the earth, and thick darkness the peoples; but the Lord will arise upon you, and his glory will be seen upon you" (Isa. 60:2, RSV). There is a darkness covering the earth. It's not getting better; it's getting worse. What I see on television these days sickens me. Sitcoms that used to be funny are now filled with perversion. For a Christian, there isn't much worth watching anymore.

The Bible says the Lord will fill all the earth with His glory. How is He going to do that? The glory of God is going to be on you, and the people are going to see it. The only glory your family and others will see is what is on you. If you're walking around depressed all the time, why would they ever want to come into the kingdom—plus give up their Sundays? If Jesus gives you no joy, and you have no fun in life, and you can't enjoy anything, I feel sorry for you. So life is hard. It was hard last week, last year. Still, the joy of the Lord is our strength.

What's God been doing in you in the last five years? It's called character development. He could have taken us right into the glory. Do you know why He didn't? Because there are generations to come.

I look back ten years and think how stupid I was then. I guess ten years from now, and until Jesus comes, I'll look back and remember how stupid I was. He has been working on my character. And He's been watching to see how you respond in certain situations. What are you doing in your marriage, with your money, at your job? Are you going to prevail and overcome? The devil tries to convince us that God wants to see how long we can dangle.

My husband often reminds me that the generous man will be made fat. In Hebrew, that means he will get the anointing; the generous man gets the anointing.

Why do we want the anointing? In it is everything we need. You don't have to have a pulpit ministry. Most of you will never have one, but you can affect people for the kingdom of God that I'll never be able to touch. You can go with the glory of God. All you have to do is walk into a room, and people will notice something about you that they just can't explain.

How do you get that glory? Pray, fast, give, and do all those other things you know to do. But the Lord has been impressing me with this—they'll know that we're Christians because we have *love*.

If in the midst of a crisis a medical team administered a new drug to your husband to save his life and then told you he had a *reaction* to the medicine, you would know that was bad news.

But if they told you that your husband *responded* to the treatment, you'd know that's good. Reaction is bad. Response is good. The Lord has been putting me in a responsive mood and taking me out of a reactive mood.

The mirrors in our bathroom extend from the sink to the ceiling. When my husband brushes his teeth, he leaves toothpaste and water spots all over the mirrors. I think he takes his brush and flings the water off it and onto the mirror. It's gross, and I hate it. You men or women who live alone, rejoice!

One day—after I brought this to Randi's attention—I walked into the bathroom and was taken aback by my water-spotted mirror. I thought, *I cook when I'm home. I also go out and minister. I take time with my children in between meetings. Why do I have to put up with this mess?*

The Lord spoke to me and said, "You want the glory. Get the Windex." You see, we think the glory comes by going to the Philippines and having water drip on our heads from a leaking roof or having a dirty outhouse to use. However, we don't all get that opportunity. So, I got the Windex.

When my husband came home that afternoon, he

said, "Honey, did you see how nice and clean I kept the mirrors?" I almost bit my tongue in half to keep from saying anything. Why? Because I want the glory of God in my life. I want God's presence with me always.

What have you been going through? I'm certain that more times than not, your suffering can be blamed on your tongue. Or your disobedience. Have you put up your fist toward God and said, "God, if You don't do something, I'll just die. If You really love me, why are You allowing this to happen to me? I wouldn't do this to someone I loved."

When I get provoked, I take it as a green light, not a red light. I've heard Christians say, "I guess this is God's way of closing the door." When I go through hard places I know I must be right on track, because the devil is really mad.

I often say, "God stops; the devil only hinders." If I recognize that I am only being hindered, I push ahead.

I know you will find this hard to believe, but Randi and I were having a disagreement. I thought I had made a good decision about something all on my own. In fact, I convinced myself (and told him) I had made the decision for *his* benefit. I felt I was justified because I was being prudent and helping *him*. I don't advise you to try this with your husband. It's not a good idea.

Randi was on a business trip when I made the monumental decision, and when he returned home he was not very happy. I reminded him of how much money I had saved us, but he was not pacified. I know this never happens in your house, but we had a little yelling session—after which I proceeded to prepare to minister at a huge, much-advertised women's conference.

I told Randi that I was leaving for a meeting and would probably never return home. (Of course he didn't buy that!) A perfect frame of mind to begin a conference, don't you think? I'm sharing this with you to let you know that you too can have a relationship with God and be used by Him even when you blow it.

I decided I couldn't leave the house in that condition. What if I got hit by a train or some other horrible thing happened to me? So I walked across the room to where my husband was sitting, knelt at his feet, put my head in his lap, and told him I was wrong in what I did. I asked him to forgive me. I was crying, because I knew I had hurt him.

When we hurt someone, we're sometimes glad because we've struck back—especially if he has hurt us. You must be able to say, "I'm sorry, I know I have hurt you."

If the person forgives you, praise God. However, he may reply, "Some things will never change. Get off my back."

Randi put his arms around me and began to weep. He said, "I just want us to be together in our decisions." And he was right. I often go out on a limb because I think I'm alone.

When I arrived at that women's conference, I felt the greatest anointing I have experienced in all my years of ministry. It didn't come by preaching the Word. That is what you can *see*. The glory comes when you can't see me. The anointing comes when you can't see Cathy Lechner as a wife and mother, cooking tuna noodle casserole for the fourth day in a row.

The Lord spoke to me and said, "As long as you will stand together in unity and keep your heart right, there isn't anything that I won't do for you. Even if you and Randi both blow it, if you will humble yourselves and stand together, I'll do it."

You see, our relationship with each other reflects our relationship with our heavenly Father. The bridge of forgiveness over which we cross to forgive our family and friends is the same bridge over which forgiveness comes to us from the Father.

If you feel all alone but humble yourself, there isn't anything God won't do for you. He resists the proud, but He gives grace to the humble.

Do you want the glory of God? It comes when you are on the front line. It comes in relationships with one another.

Can you pray right now and ask God for His glory as you walk in forgiveness to any and all who have hurt you? God has forgiven them, and so can you.

Say yes, and see the glory of God in your life. ♥

Cathy Lechner is the best-selling author of *I'm Trying to Sit at His Feet, But Who's Going to Cook Dinner?* and *Couldn't We Just Kill 'em and Tell God They Died?* (Creation House), and has been featured on TBN's *Praise the Lord* show and on *The 700 Club*. She is also a national women's minister and speaker. Cathy and her husband, Randi, reside in Jacksonville, Florida, with their six children.

Material in this chapter was taken from *Couldn't We Just Kill 'em and Tell God They Died?* (Creation House).

5

Quityerbellyaching!

by Betty Malz

T HERE IS A LEGEND passed down from the natives of the Solomon Islands in the South Pacific. When woodsmen can't fell a large tree with an ax, they "cut it down" by yelling at it. Several woodsmen with special powers creep up on the tree at dawn and scream at the top of their lungs. They continue this for thirty days. The tree dies and falls over. The theory is that the hollering over a period of time kills the spirit of the tree. According to the villagers, it always works. Words that kill.

Another legend tells of a monastery centuries ago that was nearly extinct. Only five monks were left, restless and wrangling among themselves. Suddenly an unknown visitor appeared with a message: "One of you could be the Messiah." The five began treating each other with extraordinary respect, just in case. A mighty revival broke out. Words that resurrect.

Just think how this concept could resurrect a dead marriage!

Most women talk too much. I believe some have been vaccinated with a phonograph needle—talking ninety miles per hour nonstop, most of it nagging. James 3:6 says the tongue is set on fire by hell.

Living with a woman like this is like the Chinese "death of a thousand cuts." They don't slash a man to death but torture him by using a razor blade to make a small cut on his flesh daily. He slowly seeps to death, little by little, until he is gone.

I believe marriages die this way—a jab here, a criticism there. It's like saving green stamps and then turning in the whole book of complaints, killing matrimony.

My mother used to have two little pink cards taped to her dressing table in the bedroom: "Exhort means the language of encouragement," and "Criticism cripples."

A rule of courtesy: Half of the conversation should belong to the other person. Even nagging can be put into words of positive confession.

When Carl and I were first married, he took a new job at Trinity Bible College. We played God and Moses. Moses never saw God's face, just His "hinder parts." All I ever saw of Carl was his backside, going out the door to do something good for someone else. Carl brought home his leftover charm, his leftover brain, his leftover wit and energy—after giving his best to the college students all day. When I tried to talk to him, I could tell his attention span was thin.

Once, in a monotone, I inserted, "Tuesday you will receive divorce papers from a local attorney." To which he nodded, smiled and muttered his usual at intervals—"Uh-huh, sure, OK." Suddenly, after stepping out the door onto the porch, he re-entered with a loud "What?"

It worked. I had his attention. After communicating we made a pact. I promised to talk half as much if he would listen twice as hard. That worked, too. We concluded that Carl didn't have too much to do, but I had too little. (That was before I started writing!)

Forgive your husband for not being everything you need. My husband does not like horses. Instead of complaining about this difference, I share this activity with a friend who does like horses.

You can smother each other. Two logs in a fireplace must have a little air space between them in order to burn. It's possible to be two train tracks running side by side in unity without being a monorail.

Be content. No one can make you happy. Happiness is homemade. Happiness is something you are. My grandmother told me, "Some women living in palatial homes are happy, but the happiest women usually live in tents—'Godliness with conTENTment is great gain.'"

I suggest we wives adopt Johnny Mercer's song for our theme: "You gotta accentuate the positive, eliminate the negative, latch onto the affirmative, and don't mess with Mr. In-between." This song should be on page 1 of every church hymnal and stamped at the top of every issued marriage license.

Don't criticize him in public. If you must communicate an unbearable trait, do it with a quiet, loving voice in private. If he won't listen, or if he is a better debater than you, write him a thoughtful but sincere letter.

If yours is not a workable situation, the Scripture tells us, "Having done all . . . stand" (Eph. 6:13, KJV). Some things only God can do. If your husband is still unhappy, it could be guilt from unconfessed personal sin. But don't let his unhappiness be your fault.

Quityerbellyaching! Adopt Philippians 4:8 (KJV): " . . . whatsoever things are lovely, whatsoever things are of good report . . . think on these things." Count your husband's blessings, not his shortcomings.

If you do these things, you will be surprised at your change of attitude toward him. What's more, you will change as you pray for him. ♥

6

Taking Care of Daddy

by Annie Chapman

SINCE THE TIME Nathan (now twenty-one) and Heidi (now eighteen) were infants, it's been my desire to know that the children loved and respected their father. In Malachi 4:6 (KJV) we read: "And he shall turn the heart of the fathers to the children, and the heart of the children to their fathers, lest I come and smite the earth with a curse." The lack of father-child relationships has indeed cursed this land. So to avoid that curse in our "land," I have determined to do all I can to encourage Steve's role as father.

However, at the outset of our marriage there was a question of whether children would even be a part of our future.

During the late sixties and early seventies I was influenced by the feminist movement and its ideas. As a result I was very negative about children. I felt children were just messy, noisy, bothersome little inconveniences that would hold me back from my potential. My ungodly, selfish attitude didn't seem to bother Steve. In fact, after our discussion on the matter, I thought Steve was in full agreement. Little did I know he was simply blinded by love.

When Steve's grandfather died, we went back to West Virginia for the funeral. It was to become a life-changing experience for me. Steve's grandfather had fathered eleven children: eight sons and three daughters. I sat in that funeral home and watched them come and go. Dozens and dozens of what would become hundreds of people who were the offspring of George Stonewall Chapman and his wife, Easter. Later that evening while driving home I thought about how many people had come from that one couple, and that Grandpa Chapman would never really die, for he lived on in his children and his children's children. It was at that moment the Lord said to me, "Steve is an honorable man. I want him to live on in his children."

That shook me. Right then I repented of my hard heart and resolved to allow God to change my mind. Mercifully over a period of time He did renovate my heart and mind and thus made room for the addition of children to our family.

What can a mother do to help her husband become a good daddy? It is important to realize, before anything else is said on this subject, that as mothers we cannot and should not take on the responsibility for the relationship between father and child. We are not our husband's Holy Spirit. For that reason we should not try to nag our husbands into the Papa Hall of Fame. But how can we encourage and strengthen that essential bond between father and children?

First of all, we can give Dad the chance to learn to be a good father.

I remember the first time I left Nathan alone with Steve. Nathan was just a couple of weeks old when I had an opportunity to go strawberry picking with friends. I hadn't been our of the house for what seemed decades, so I jumped at the chance. Steve was left in charge of our precious son. As I went out the door I called back over my shoulder, "Honey, if he needs changing, you go ahead and change him." I learned later that Steve was hoping I was talking about changing his personality or something—anything but "that."

About three hours later I arrived back home. I walked in to find Nathan screaming at the top of his lungs, wet, dirty—rather neglected. Giving Steve a nasty look, I set out to put my baby's life back in order.

Steve explained apologetically that he had gotten involved in writing a song. He said he was just about to tend to Nathan when I walked in. Sensing I was upset with him, Steve pleaded insanity. I believed him.

In all truth, Steve is a terrific father. But he's still a lousy mother. He is not aware of some of the details I feel are important, like brushing teeth and changing underwear. But when it comes to having a good time with the kids and making them feel special, Steve can't be beat.

That brings up my second point. We need to allow our husbands the freedom to be the kind of father they want to be rather than the kind of father we want them to be.

My idea of some extra-special time between Steve and the children would be a rousing game of Scrabble. Building a roaring fire in the fireplace, making some hot chocolate and settling down for a winner-takes-all board game is what life is all about—to me.

Steve has other ideas. A truly meaningful time spent with Nathan consists of the two of them waking up at 3:00 A.M., facing sub-zero weather, packing an arsenal of weapons, and going out to annihilate some poor little bunny or—worse yet—Bambi's cousin.

As the wife and mother of these would-be great hunters, I have found it necessary to keep my mouth shut. I was sharing with a friend of mine how worried I get when Steve and Nathan are in the woods during hunting season. I told her it was like sending my baby boy into a shooting gallery with a bull's eye painted on his forehead.

My friend said, "I would give anything just to get my husband out of the house. I want him to take the kids hiking and camping; instead, he plays games all the time."

Whether a father is more like Daniel Boone or Daniel Webster, he needs the freedom to be the kind of father he is most comfortable being.

Another time I have to keep my mouth shut is when it's time for one of his infamous "dates" with Heidi. Just the mere mention of going out on a date with her father sends Heidi into a frenzy of preparation. Where Nathan enjoys the woods and rough-and-tumble activities, Heidi's idea of "roughing it" is to have access to an indoor pool or room service.

From the time she was a toddler, Heidi and Steve have "dated." Steve gets all dressed up with tie and jacket. Heidi wears her finest Sunday dress, and off they go to a nice restaurant. In the past Steve has always given Heidi her choice of places to eat. When she was younger, they had MacWonderful times, but now that she's older her tastes have been upscaled. The size of the checks has increased also.

So I bite my tongue and put into practice my third point. We must demonstrate, in word and deed, love and respect for Dad.

Our children are like policemen. They always have their radar on. They are always aware of what's happening ahead. No matter what we may preach or teach, they know the real score. If we tell them to respect and love their father, yet they sense disgust and disdain in our actions, their radar gives them an accurate reading. At this point our words mean nothing, for our actions speak so loudly they can't hear a word we're saying.

The most important thing we can do as mothers to help nurture the father-child relationship is to *show* love and respect for their father.

Our verbal affirmations are very important. From the time the children were infants I have consistently and constantly told them of Steve's great love for the Lord and for his family. But it can't stop there. Our actions must be consistent with our words.

If I don't treat Steve with respect and trust his

decisions, why should Nathan and Heidi? The big decisions are important, but the groundwork is laid in the everyday type of decisions.

For example, on Sundays after church the decision of whether we eat out is left entirely up to Steve. I always give him the option of eating at home or going to a restaurant. I'll say, "Steve, do you want to go home and have peanutbutter-tuna sandwiches or go out to lunch?" The decision is his. I've noticed the children never even question this arrangement. Perhaps it's because I am at peace with whatever decision Steve makes. Believe it or not, he sometimes opts for eating at home.

Proverbs 14:1 says, "The wise woman builds her house, but the foolish tears it down with her own hands." As wise women, wives, and mothers, we need to be about the business of building up those we love. ♥

Annie Chapman is best known for her music ministry with her husband, Steve Chapman. Called "musical ambassadors to the family," they have been singing together about real-life family situations for over twenty years. During that time they have recorded several albums and co-written *Married Lovers, Married Friends; Gifts Your Kids Can't Break; Running On Empty (and Looking for the Nearest Exit); Smart Women Keep It Simple* (all with Bethany House); as well as Steve's latest book, *A Look at Life From a Deerstand* (Harvest House). The Chapmans won the Dove award in 1988 for best in country gospel music. Steve and Annie live in Pleasant View, Tennessee.

7

Six Ways to Say "I Love You"

by Betty Malz

WHETHER A MAN is a refined, educated dandy or a homegrown boy from the hills of Kentucky, his basic needs remain the same. Here are six steps you, as his wife, can take to meet them:

1. Let him know he is your *primary* interest.
2. Avoid *criticism* like leprosy.
3. Stress *simplicity.*
4. *Honor* him.
5. Practice *total commitment/unconditional love.*
6. Apply the *Golden Rule.*

Primary interest: We must consider his daily homecoming important and groom ourselves before his arrival.

My friend Dawn Wagler is a busy artist and writer. Her husband is director of a camp in Illinois. They have children to care for, but she told me, "I don't put on a satin formal for his return home in the evening, but I manage to be clean, comfortably and attractively dressed, and even if I'm elbow deep in dishwater or bent over diapering a baby, I acknowledge his coming through the door with excited anticipation and loving attention. I think it's important to clear the air of any tension or anxiety so that he comes into a welcoming, relaxed atmosphere. Sometimes I light candles for the table, even if the meal is simple."

All men and most women enjoy good food. So serve his meals on time. Even if you can't be pretty, you can be punctual. I've learned never to discuss business, controversial issues, or kid problems on an empty stomach. Or to serve Carl leftovers—leftover food, leftover time, leftover energy, or leftover charm.

Let me stress the importance of being dependable and predictable. Avoid teeter-totter moods. On the other hand, men like surprises. Show him attention in private and in public. On an impulse, kiss his cheek while riding in the car, hold his hand in church. Write him notes and put them in his briefcase, on the steering wheel of his car, on his Bible, in his lunchbox, or on his computer. You might even mail them to his office. He'll get the message: "I'll never be bored with her."

Instant family success is not available like instant chocolate breakfast. Work at it. Let it happen.

Avoid personal criticism: If he doesn't know how to dress, keep your mouth shut and your billfold open. Buy him things that make him look attractive.

My sister-in-law Bobbie told me of a couple who is still in love after thirty-one years of marriage. She is better educated than he and two inches taller. But *he doesn't know he is short.* He is nine feet tall inside because she honors, respects, and reveres him and takes care of her personal appearance *for him.*

Recently in a crowd I overheard a lady describe her mate: "He's that short, compact-sized male sitting by the window." If she wants to be loved in return, she must ignore his "short-comings."

In Idaho they have an annual fiddlers' contest. Contestants even come from Japan. The judges are put in an isolated room where they cannot see the fiddlers, but only hear their music.

One of the judges said, "We don't care if you're stark naked and wear a bone in your nose. If you can fiddle, it's all right with us. It's the music that counts."

Looks help, but in marriage we must develop personality, soul, sense of humor, and spirit—things that outlast looks and youth, things that don't wear out but get finer with the using. It's the music that counts.

Simplicity: Life was meant to be sipped, not gulped. In the beginning Satan beguiled Adam and Eve's simplicity (2 Cor. 11:3). I might add, he has been complicating the lives of married couples ever since. Don't crowd life.

I am a writer, speaker, organist, wife, mother—but when I want to say "I love you," I sacrifice some time to bake a pan of warm cornbread for Carl. Little things mean a lot to him, and to all men.

One of our neighbors told us, "My wife only

cooks about one meal a month. I can feed all three members of our family for three days for what it costs us to eat out once." You can make a car payment on what it takes to eat out all the time. Let eating out be a special occasion, not routine.

One simple thing I do about once a month is fix Carl's favorite meal.

Honor: Here are three cardinal rules: Don't blab, don't tell personal secrets, treat him as well as you would treat a guest.

First Peter 3:7–13 admonishes us to honor our mates. If we don't our prayers will be hindered.

Be compassionate and courteous. If you do not pay back evil for evil and don't quarrel, you will inherit a blessing. If you refrain from dishonoring your mate, you will love life! Follow this rule, and no one can harm you. The eyes of the Lord will be over you. You will be happy. You will avoid terror. And your "land" will not be troubled.

Romans 12:10 tells us to be kindly affectioned to one another, to prefer one another in honor.

Talk to your husband as considerately as you would to a paying customer. Treat him with the same respect you do your boss. Bite your tongue. Ask yourself, Would I talk to my neighbor or business associate the way I talk to my husband?

Commitment/unconditional love: Some women are hitchhikers. They stroll along the bridal path, hitchhiking until a better ride comes along. Commitment is essential to a secure marriage and the children involved. *Never* use the words *divorce, split,* or *separate.* The devil will capitalize on that negative confession from your mouth.

Some girls look at their man during the wedding

ceremony at the altar, and say to themselves, *I will alter him.* Commitment is a must. Each male comes labeled "As is."

Roberta Gould is a writer who is married to a creative music director of a large church. She has found that she must be a shock absorber, especially on Sunday, his busiest day. This is not the same as a doormat, but a helpmate.

Roberta tries to absorb any conflict with the children. And she supports her husband with the praise and approval that musicians thrive on in order to keep producing. She says that more than once she has absorbed the blame or written a note to say "sorry" for a disagreement, even when it wasn't totally her fault.

On Sunday she arranges an hour of quiet, uninterrupted time for him. She serves fluffy mashed potatoes because it is one of his favorite dishes. By Monday the return of her investment is realized. He listens to her and values her opinions. She is rewarded for absorbing his anxieties on his difficult day by maintaining a steady week.

Joanne Bunce is the pastor of a thriving church in Niagara Falls, New York. She says "I love you" to her busy husband, Ted, by making him chili, homemade strawberry shortcake, and a pot of coffee served in front of the television. She has maintained a busy career and loving marriage for thirty-nine years. She also says "I love you" by letting him collect and store what she terms junk. He calls them curios and antiques. Sometimes, as much as she hates the stuff, she shows her love for Ted by going to a flea market and buying something for his collection. She says, "I become richer when he responds with appreciation and unrestrained glee."

Unconditional love is stronger than super glue.

Apply the Golden Rule: The maxim "Do unto others as you would have them do unto you" should be applied to marriage. Scripture admonishes us: "You shall love the Lord your God with all your heart, and with all your soul and with all your mind . . . You shall love your neighbor as yourself" (Matt. 22: 37, 39). If we would love God first and then love our mates as much as we love ourselves, there would be no inequality in marriage but rather unity and a sacred, loving bond.

A woman was walking along the ocean's shoreline when she stumbled onto a bottle with a genie in it! The genie promised her one wish.

"I have always been afraid to fly. Before I die, I want to go to Hawaii. Would you build me a highway so I can drive there instead of flying?"

The genie thought a minute, then reasoned, "It would take a lot of cement and oh so many pilings. I don't think this wish would be possible. What is your second wish?"

The woman pleaded, "That I could understand my husband."

The genie was quick with his decision, "Would you like a four-lane highway or a six-lane highway?"

Conclusion: Maturity is to suffer without complaining and to be misunderstood without explaining. Try it, you'll like it. ♥

Part Two

Be a Source of Strength

_8_

Respect Him

by LeeAnn Rawlins

However, each one of you also must love his wife as he loves himself, and *the wife must respect her husband.*"

So admonishes the apostle Paul in Ephesians 5:33 (NIV, italics mine). Husbands must *love* their wives. As wives, we must love our husbands, too, but Paul makes it clear in this passage that *respecting* our husbands is of tremendous importance. Loving our husbands and respecting them are two sides of the same coin.

Women want to be loved and to feel they have a secure position in the center of their man's affections. Men also want to be loved—but even more, they want to be respected. If we can accept and understand this basic difference between the sexes, our marriages will be transformed.

What does it mean to respect your husband? *Strong's Exhaustive Concordance of the Bible* defines the Greek meaning of respect this way: "to be in awe." In some versions of the Bible it is translated "reverence." Are you in awe of your mate? Can you say that you reverence him? Yet this is a direct command from the Lord through Paul!

In practical terms, how do you show respect for your husband? One important way I've learned is to make him a priority in your life—above your work, your homemaking, your church work, even your children. The Bible says a husband and wife become one flesh, yet so often we don't respect that "other part" of us. We treat him as if he's a separate, secondary entity, sometimes without even realizing it.

When Willard and I were nearing our tenth anniversary, he came in after one particularly long, hard day, looked me in the eyes and said, "We really need to get away together, just you and me."

"That sounds wonderful!" I said. Then I began to think. What about our boys? At that time we had a new baby, our third son. How could he and the others get along without us—without me?

I smiled gingerly at Willard. "Why don't we take the kids along with us?"

His smile faded. He loved his sons very much, but he wanted to know I desired to be with just him. I could read the disappointment in his face.

Over the next few days I struggled with the conflicting feelings that warred within me. The boys needed me. But so did Willard. Finally I made a decision: I arranged to leave the children in the capable hands of close friends, and with some trepidation I left with Willard for a short trip to San Francisco.

We had a wonderful time. I still remember riding the cable cars, laughing and enjoying San Francisco Bay. One night Willard presented me with a new ring. I felt so special, and so did he. We were together again in ways we had not been in a long time.

This was just the beginning of a new and wonderful relationship. That weekend we made a choice to honor and prefer being with each other rather than living in separate worlds—me wrapped up in motherhood, and Willard in making our farm a success.

I learned a new meaning of respect: putting him first. I also learned that being a good mother did not mean giving up being a good wife. It was painful to hear Willard tell me that weekend that he felt I had stopped putting him first in my life. It seemed to him I was expending all my energies on the boys. Somewhere along the way I had stopped preferring him, *respecting* him. How easy it is to fall into this trap! But I found that, while some old habits die hard, it really doesn't take much effort or time to do the little things that communicate your respect for your husband. Weekly date nights. Little notes in his lunch. Candlelight dinners. Be creative! For me, it became important to make sure Willard and I always sat next to each other—with the boys on either side of us—when we were in the car, at church, or at the dinner table. A little thing, but it meant a lot.

I wanted to do something special for Willard's next birthday to let him know how much I loved him, so I asked the Lord to make me extra creative.

Planning was fun. I bought a simple little notebook (I remember selecting just the right one). Each day, from then until his birthday, which was nearly a year away, I would write a few lines telling him how and why I loved and respected him.

I kept my journal daily. I have to be honest, though, and say there were a few days when I just couldn't find anything positive to write. On those days I would read all the good things from the other days. This turned out to be a help and a blessing to me. It built up my love and respect for him. As the months passed and his birthday approached, the anticipation grew.

I watched Willard's eyes as he unwrapped that precious little book on that special birthday. He chuckled at my honesty when I told him about the blank pages. He was greatly moved to read about himself as seen through my eyes. It was just one of those things that can build up your husband's self-respect and make him a better person.

Respect is shown in actions—but it is also shown in words. Proverbs 18:21 (NIV) tells us, "The tongue has the power of life and death." Does that mean you can bring life or death to your husband and marriage by what you say? Yes, indeed!

Relationships need reassurance. In my relationship with Willard, I learned to praise him often. The words, "Honey, you're the best!" just can't be used too frequently. I told Willard often that I was glad I married him, that I appreciated his hard work on behalf of the family, that he was a success in my eyes. Through my praise I communicated my respect for him and made him feel special. I also increased his respect in the eyes of our children.

This is crucial, for children emulate what they see. When a child feels that his parents respect each other, he feels secure, and it is easier for him to respect them both. The opposite is also true. Disrespectful, insecure children are often the products of marriages in which the husband and wife don't have mutual respect.

Speak well of your husband—not only to your children, but to others as well. Respect is closely intertwined with a wife's submission to her husband. She must truly honor him from her heart. When a wife undermines or demeans her husband, she completely violates the true spirit of submission. A man wants a glad response from his wife to his leadership given in a natural and consistent way. When a man finds a woman with these qualities, one who is also full of great value and feminine strength, he truly finds a rare gem. In Proverbs 31:23 it says that the husband of a godly wife is "respected at the city gate"—he's respected in the community because of his wife's good reports about him. Do your friends and family respect your husband because of what you say about him? Or do they mostly see his flaws because of your frequent complaints against him? For many people you are your husband's only representative.

Show respect for him in the way you talk about him. This will have a way of getting back around to him—and to you.

I will never forget what one of Willard's best friends shared with me after Willard's death. He and Willard had gone on a fishing trip to Alaska and were sitting by the campfire with their fishing guide. When Willard got up to go to his tent, the

51

guide turned to our friend and said, "That Willard sure is a quiet one. But one thing I know about him—he really loves his wife."

I don't know what Willard said about me to that stranger. But I do know this: Respect produces respect. If you *want* respect, *give* respect. You can't lose.

Another key to respecting your husband is prayer. Don't share your concerns about your husband with your friends, neighbors, or children; take them to God in prayer. The Lord, in His wisdom, will help to bring about the needed changes in your husband, or in you.

When we fail to pray, we become frustrated with our husbands. And frustration, for so many of us, leads to nagging. Nagging is the epitome of disrespect. It is an evident sign that prayer has been neglected, and that a wife is trying to solve a spiritual problem in the flesh. The husband usually turns a deaf ear to his wife, and so she nags some more. It is a vicious cycle and frustrating for both partners.

You may think, *I'm not a nag. I'm gentle in the things I suggest. Surely my husband knows that I love him.* But that overlooks the basic difference in motivations between men and women: Women want to be loved; men want to be respected. Nagging, or even dropping subtle hints, reflects a lack of acceptance of your mate—a lack of respect. Even if the suggestion seems innocent to you, it can hurt your relationship with your husband.

However, in prayer a wife is released from a nagging spirit because she can be honest with God. She can trust in God's power to do what she cannot do. It is the world that says we must solve our own problems. God says to bring our problems to Him in prayer. Prayer can resolve more difficulties than any humanistic remedy.

When we stop nagging and complaining and start praying, respecting, and loving, we are releasing God's Spirit to work in powerful ways. Our heavenly Father's desires us to have happier, more meaningful marriages. We need to give Him the freedom and the time to work in our husband's lives, and in ours.

Let's be honest. Some of us are married to men who are more difficult to respect than others. If you're one of those wives with a hard-to-respect husband, I encourage you. Don't just bail out of a difficult situation. God loves your husband. He is of infinite value to God. Realizing this should help to make your efforts much more worthwhile.

Respect assumes acceptance—and forgiveness. Determine to establish an attitude that reflects Paul's statement in 1 Corinthians 13:5: "Love . . . keeps no record of wrongs" (NIV). So many wives seem to keep long, negative accounts of the irritating or hurtful things their husbands have done. It's as if there were tributaries in our lives that we pollute with our ugly accounts, which then flow into the rivers of our marriages until finally there is nothing but bitter, dirty water—a cesspool of "wrongs" from which nothing good can come.

It is inevitable that two people living together are going to hurt each other now and then. That's life. But we must have forgiving hearts. The longer our rivers remain polluted, the more rotten the water becomes, destroying our respect for our husbands. But forgiveness clears the river. It may be humanly impossible to *forget* completely. But the miracle of forgiveness must be applied again and again, every time the memory of an offense comes back to our minds.

Decide right now to respect your husband. Make a choice. Write out a list of your husband's good points, then make it a priority to share your list with him. Give him room to be himself without the pressure of your expectations constantly before him, and encourage him to explore all that he is and can become. Then cheer him on in the process.

Goethe, the German author, once wrote: "If you treat a man as he is, he will stay as he is, but if you treat him as if he were what he ought to be and could be, he will become that bigger and better man." It's up to you. If you believe that your man is a good husband and you treat him as a good husband, he will become a good or better husband.

Respect and love—they go hand in hand. Love your husband. Respect him. And expect a new, exciting relationship to unfold. ♥

LeeAnn Rawlins and her husband, Duane, have been married eleven years. Both lost their first mates to death after many years of being happily married. In addition to teaching worldwide for Youth With A Mission, together they conduct a marriage and family seminar called Right Choices in Marriage. Duane has two sons and a daughter. LeeAnn has three sons. Together they have fourteen grandchildren. The Rawlins live on the Youth With A Mission base in Salem, Oregon. LeeAnn is author of *Loving Your Husband for Life,* published by Creation House. She and her husband, Duane also co-authored *Raising Kids in a World Gone Wrong.*

9

Pray With Him

by Frances Hunter

WHEN GOD MADE Charles and me "one" through marriage, He gave us the right to the greatest happiness in the world. There is no beauty or state of being on earth to compare with a marriage that God makes and keeps together. Charles and I enjoy doing *everything* together—and why shouldn't we? God in His original plan created man and woman from the same flesh because He intended for our desires, our ambitions, our aims, our hopes, our likes, and our loves to be the same.

There are many ways by which oneness is partially achieved. All the things you do together—attending functions together, spending recreation time together, working in the yard together, discussing finances together and disciplining the children together—are helpful toward the goal of total oneness. But I want to concentrate on one thing that can bring more genuine oneness than anything else.

Praying Together

THERE WAS A TIME when I couldn't imagine prayer as being exciting. Maybe you feel that way now. But probably the greatest and closest times Charles and I have are those when we are praying together for the things on our hearts.

Many couples pray at the side of their bed. We have prayed there upon occasion, but our most intimate, personal, fervent prayers are those when we are wrapped in each other's arms as we lie in bed together. This is the very last thing we do at night before we go to sleep because we want God so very close to us at the close of our day.

We thank God for the fabulous day He has given us. We always have lots to talk to Him about and lots of things to thank Him for. After we finish rejoicing with Him, we pray for the requests that come to our minds concerning the people with whom we have come in contact during the day—who either need to know the Lord or who need a closer walk with Him.

As the Holy Spirit brings into our minds the conversations and letters of the day, we pray for our children and for those who have shared their burdens with us over the telephone. We pray for those who have shared their heartbreak with us through letters and for those we have shared the plan of salvation with during the day. We pray for business and household needs. We pray for specific needs in the churches in which we have spoken. We pray for our future engagements—for the churches we'll be going to. We pray for whatever book we are writing currently. We pray for the areas of our lives that need improving.

We don't have any particular order of prayer at bedtime, but we just pray as God's Holy Spirit leads us. Many times we thank God for bringing us a fresh, new message from His Word. There are so many, many things to thank Him for. We have also discovered that by saying the words "God, I love You," or "I love You, Jesus" audibly we receive a fresh awareness of God, and it brings the presence of God so near that no one could ever doubt He is right in the room with us.

Practicing the presence of God is such a precious experience—especially when the lights are out, the house is quiet, and there's a stillness that seems to make it easier to hear God. As Charles and I lie in each other's arms and pray, we ask God to wrap His arms of love around our arms of love and keep us safe through the night.

The most wonderful way in the world to go to sleep is knowing that God's arms are wrapped around both of ours. There's a closeness to God that's supernatural, and there's an intimacy and closeness between a married couple that really can't be achieved any other way. Somehow God's power strips away the veneer of our lives, and in our honesty to God we become even more honest with each other. As we draw closer to Him, we draw closer to each other and become truly one.

If there is any hostility or misunderstanding between a couple, there's no better way to break it down than through prayer in each other's arms. God is so forgiving that you can't help but be in the same forgiving mood when you're talking to Him with your arms around your mate. Consequently, hostility or misunderstanding—when lifted to God—becomes an apology to the other person. And since it's filtered through God, the beauty of the moment is unsurpassed.

Oftentimes as we are praying at night, the Holy Spirit brings into my mind something I may have forgotten to tell Charles, and as I talk to God about it, Charles hears too. There's something about night prayer that brings all the things of the day into recall. What more blessed way is there to relax than talking to the One who cared enough to let His Son die for us? Just to know the power of God's love is the best sleeping pill I know of, and what a beautiful way to slip into sleep—with God.

Although I've concentrated on praying in bed, that is not the only place we pray! Charles and I pray constantly as things come up. We don't wait for night to fall. The time to pray for any request is at the moment it arises.

The other night at the supper table Charles bit his tongue, and even though we had to laugh a little as we were praying, we asked God to stop the bleeding and the pain. *Instantly* it left. We didn't wait to see what was going to happen; we just put down our knives and forks and prayed right on the spot.

I think many problems in marriages exist because people don't depend on God for *everything*. When something happens, they don't take it to God in prayer. They're really dependent on themselves, not God. The fact that Charles and I share every prayer burden with each other means that our closeness to each other grows each day. Besides, when we're concerned for each other's needs and the needs of other people, there's no time to criticize each other. Because we look to God for everything, we have found that problems just don't come up that might be a source of irritation in our marriage.

How do you start this kind of relationship? Maybe you have never prayed together—and when I say "together," I mean "out loud." Maybe you have a reservation about doing this. May I suggest you start right now, or whenever your husband is home next? Just hold hands and say, "Thank You, Lord, for making him my husband."

You don't know what it will do to your relationship with God, and you can't imagine what it will do to your marriage.

What if you have never prayed aloud? How do you start? First of all, it helps if both of you are interested in making your marriage really exciting. You won't have a communication gap, and it won't be as hard on you as it will be on those couples who aren't in agreement. Talk to each other, and suggest that you start talking to God nightly. One of you will have to start it—and while it should be the husband, if he's not the prayer warrior in your house, you be the one to begin.

But keep one thing in mind: The male ego is strong. If neither of you has made a practice of praying aloud, your husband may not want to admit his weakness in this area. So while you may have to start the praying, don't show off. Make it simple and very, very short.

Then say, "Honey, you've just got to help me."

Ask him to give you some ideas as to what you should pray about.

Remember while this is going on that God is real and is eager to hear from you. Think of prayer in this manner: If some friends that you and your husband hadn't seen for some time dropped in to visit, you would tell them what had happened since you last saw them, wouldn't you? Try talking to God that way—just as you would with a friend.

The trouble with too many couples who don't pray together is they wait too long to begin praying. They wait until their marriage is close to hitting the rocks. Then, in a last-minute flurry to hold things together, the wife decides that prayer is the answer. Maybe the husband will hardly listen to her by this time. Perhaps he will reject almost anything she suggests. As a result, one or the other or both will be annoyed. But even if you are annoyed to the limit with your husband, I dare you to go up to him, hold hands and say, "God, will You let my husband know I love him even though we are mad at each other?"

I guarantee you won't be mad by the time you finish praying—it just can't be done. There's something about God that brings love into a relationship and diminishes anger.

If yours is one of those marriages in which you have waited longer than you should have waited to start praying, just imagine God's smiling on you right now and saying, "I'm so glad you're going to start talking to Me about your problems. I've been waiting for such a long time for this because I know the solution. And don't worry about what you say to Me. You don't have to be clever or trained. The only thing I want from you is your willingness to call on Me, knowing that My love can solve the greatest problems. Now, My child, what did you want to tell Me?"

You see, that's the way God really feels. He wants His children to be happy. He wants us to talk to Him so He can give us the answers to the things that bog us down. Because God is a giving God, He longs to give! He wants to give you the special warmth of His love. He wants to heal your broken heart and give you peace. He wants to get rid of the communication gap and all the other things that keep a marriage from being perfect.

It's futile when we try to run our house without God. We always run into trouble. Listen to what the Bible says: "Unless the Lord builds the house, they labor in vain who build it; unless the Lord guards the city, the watchman keeps awake in vain, It is vain for you to rise up early, to retire late, to eat the bread of painful labors; for He gives to His beloved even in his sleep" (Ps. 127:12).

Unless the Lord builds your house, you labor in vain and worry all night long. Think of the sleepless nights in homes that have been built without God. But to His beloved, God gives sleep.

There have been times when Charles or I have fallen asleep while the other was praying in bed because we have been so blanketed with the peace of God it was impossible to stay awake. The one praying didn't get offended but eventually fell off to sleep in peace too.

Try praying for oneness, will you? ♥

Frances Hunter and her husband, Charles Hunter, at a combined age of 158 years, continue to conduct healing services throughout the world, are the authors of forty-seven books, and have ministered in forty-nine nations, and are now coordinating a World Evangelistic Census—door-by-door evangelism under the leadership of pastors to "preach the gospel of salvation to every creature on earth." They love each other and they love Jesus! They have celebrated their twenty-eighth wedding anniversary and, in their words, "we have still never had an argument, fight, or a cross word."

Adapted from *How to Make Your Marriage Exciting* by Charles and Frances Hunter, Hunter Books.

_10_

Pray for Him

by Jean Coleman

I ROLLED OVER in the bed and wrapped my arms around my sleeping husband. It was time for my nightly "laying on of hands" for his salvation. Daily he resisted my efforts to lead him to the Lord, refusing to have anything to do with spiritual things. But he couldn't stop me from praying, and I was determined to pray him into the kingdom. What a great man of God he was going to be someday! By faith I could see him preaching and teaching, healing the sick and casting out demons. I could see us moving as one in the ministry. I knew the Lord was going to save him in answer to my prayers.

He stirred slightly as I placed my hand on his chest: "O God," I pleaded, "give him a heart to seek after You and the things of the kingdom." I moved my hands up to his ears. "Give him ears to hear Your voice." Again I shifted my hands. "And a mouth filled with the Word of God." Ever so gently I touched his eyes with my fingertips, "Give Jack the eyes to see Your glory, and renew him in the spirit of his mind."

Love and faith rose up within me. If I loved my husband this much, imagine how much the Lord must love him! There was no doubt that he would be saved. The Word of God declared it: "Believe in the Lord Jesus, and you shall be saved, you and your household" (Acts 16:31). God was going to do it! My faith stood strong.

It wasn't always easy to stand strong in faith. If I looked with my natural eyes it often seemed that Jack was moving farther away from God rather than closer. We were unequally yoked and pulling in opposite directions.

One day things came to a head. Jack pulled his suitcases from the attic and informed me he was moving out.

"If I had wanted a preacher for a wife, I would have married one," he shouted. "You're no fun anymore. All you want to do is pray, read the Bible, and go to church. I've had it up to here with you and your Jesus."

As he stormed from the kitchen toward the bedroom to pack, I felt as if my heart were breaking. My marriage had always been my most cherished treasure. From the time I was a little girl all I had ever wanted was a husband and family. And now it was all crumbling before my eyes.

I leaned my head against the refrigerator and cried out to God, "Lord, You know how much I love him, but even if it costs me my marriage, I'm not turning back." The die had been cast. Jesus had to come first in my life no matter what the cost. "I'm not turning back"—it was the prayer of relinquishment, the prayer of total commitment to the call of God.

I felt a hand on my shoulder. I turned. It was Jack. "I've decided to stay," he said. "I may not like you anymore, but I still love you."

With those words, he headed up the stairs to put his suitcases away. It was the testing of my faith. Like Abraham of old, I had to place the one I loved on the altar. And, like Abraham, I received him back.

Through that experience I also received the gift of faith to believe for Jack's salvation no matter what happened. Our marriage ran through some rough waters, but I'm convinced my prayers of faith served as a life jacket. They were keeping Jack afloat until he decided to reach out to the Savior himself. I knew he was going to be saved, and I refused to allow him to sink.

Praying the prayer of faith is one thing. Waiting for the answer is quite another. I liken it to the long nine months of pregnancy a woman must endure until the actual birth of the child. As the months drag along, the waiting gets harder and harder. We want to rush things, even induce early labor. But it is so important to wait for the fullness of time. Premature babies are often weak and sickly and can even die. How much better to wait the full term.

Jack's gestation period was sixteen months. One weekend he expressed a desire to go to church with me. I could hardly believe it! And less than five minutes after the service began, he asked Jesus to reign in his life as Savior and Lord. The minister didn't even give an invitation. As Jack sat in the presence of God, he opened his heart to Him. God had answered my prayer in His time and in His way.

I have always believed that if you pray little prayers, you will get little answers, but if you pray big prayers, you can expect big answers. So with the miracle of Jack's salvation acting as a real faith-booster, I began to pray that the Lord would raise him up as a mighty man of God. I prayed that the Lord would open doors of ministry where he would touch the lives of thousands of people and that together we would carry the name of Jesus to the uttermost parts of the earth.

Several weeks later my husband informed me he had volunteered to work with a local television ministry. I rejoiced! I was sure the Lord had answered my prayer, and in my mind's eye I could see him reaching millions of souls for Jesus as a televangelist. I was in for a real surprise.

Instead of heading off to the television studio, Jack set up an office in the corner of our dark, damp basement. It turned out that he was going to handle all the mailing for the television program—sending out Bibles and tracts that were requested by viewers. Every night he would retire to his workroom to spend hours reading letters, stuffing envelopes, and licking stamps.

I had a lot to learn about praying in the Spirit. How great is the wisdom of God! Given my way, I would have thrust a novice into a major ministry. But God was teaching Jack a very important lesson: how to be a servant. For several years he would be hidden away in the desert of the basement as he met with God and proved himself faithful in the little things. God was answering my prayer—just not the way I expected.

Nor did I expect the phone call that came one day informing me that Jack was having a heart attack and was being rushed to the hospital. I could hardly believe it.

As I stood by the hospital bed gazing down at my husband's ashen face, all I could pray was, "O God, do something."

And I heard the Lord respond, "I want *you* to do something. I want you to praise Me for the healing I am going to bring to Jack."

It didn't seem like the time to praise. Jack's heart was broken, and mine was breaking. But in obedience I declared, "I praise You, Jesus!" There was a stirring in my spirit, I repeated the words a second time, "I praise You, Jesus. You are worthy to be praised."

Faith welled up from deep within me, and praises flowed out from me. "Jesus, You are our healer! You are the One who heals the brokenhearted. There's nothing too hard for You!"

As I praised the Lord, I knew Jack was going to be all right. Externally, nothing had changed. The monitor still bleeped out his irregular heartbeat. But I was now seeing through eyes of faith. He was going to get well! God was going to heal him!

I squeezed Jack's hand. "You're going to be fine. Don't worry about anything. Jesus is going to heal you completely."

All doubt was gone.

Just at that moment the door opened, and the

doctor stepped in. I could sense his concern by the grave expression on his face. As he approached my husband's bed, suddenly Jack's mouth turned up into a radiant smile.

"Don't worry, doctor," he said. "I'm going to be fine. Jesus is healing me, and there are going to be no further problems with my heart."

"We'll just have to see about that," the doctor responded.

A few days later Jack was discharged from the hospital. No heart damage, no restrictions, no special treatments. He was healed and ready to be about the Father's business.

God was also ready to answer my many prayers asking that Jack and I might serve him together in ministry, only once again not the way I expected.

"The Lord has been telling me that we are to raise up a church here in Laurel," Jack said one afternoon.

A church? A *local* church? I had certainly never prayed to be a pastor's wife. I had no interest in Sunday school programs and nurseries. I had asked God to allow Jack and me to travel around the world and win thousands of souls to Jesus. The last thing in the world I wanted to do was start a church in my own hometown. I refused even to entertain the thought.

Over the next few weeks my husband continued to press the church issue. I fought him every step of the way, closing my heart and mind completely to such an outlandish idea. Start a church? It was out of the question.

Finally one day Jack pointed a finger at me and said, "You are the most stubborn woman I have ever met. If Jesus Himself were to stand here and command you to start a church, you would still refuse it."

As he walked away, I hung my head in shame. I knew Jack was right. I had prayed for the Lord to raise him up into a mighty man of God—and then I had resisted the very answer to those prayers. With tears streaming down my cheeks, I surrendered my will to God. More than anything else I wanted to be in the center of His will, and if that meant sacrificing my dreams and ambitions—so be it.

Today Jack and I travel thousands of miles to the uttermost parts of the earth preaching the gospel side by side in conferences and crusades. The Lord who made us one is using us as one to share the marvelous love of Jesus. My prayers for Jack have been answered. And in the process God has given me the desires of my heart too.

Many years have passed since those nights I used to lie in bed and pray for God to save my husband. But I still wrap my arms around him every night and cover him with prayer. Occasionally Jack will sense that I am praying and stir in his sleep. He will reach for my hand, give it a gentle squeeze and mumble sleepily, "Thanks for your prayers."

And then we both fall asleep wrapped in the everlasting arms of God. ♥

Jean Coleman and her husband, Jack, are the founders of The Tabernacle, an international Christian center located in Laurel, Maryland. After serving as co-pastors of their church for nearly twenty years, the Colemans recently stepped out of the pastorate into a global ministry that carries them to the uttermost parts of the earth. Their hearts are especially linked to the nation of India. They are also being used to encourage church leadership in the United States through their unique "team ministry" method of practical teaching and exhortation. Jean is a freelance writer whose articles have appeared in *Ministries Today* and numerous other Christian publications. She continues to be in demand as a conference speaker both at home and abroad. Her newsletter, *The Pastor's Helpmate,* has been read by thousands of pastors' wives around the world.

11

Encourage Him

by Michele Buckingham

M<small>Y HUSBAND AND</small> I had been married only a few months when we were faced with our first crisis. Bruce, who worked in a congressional office in Washington, D.C., was "encouraged" to find another job. He wasn't fired—just given a deadline of two months to relocate. The congressman he worked for inherited the chairmanship of a space science subcommittee, and with it a built-in staff. Bruce's services were no longer needed.

It was difficult news for us. Our new townhouse in the Maryland suburbs was small but cozy— with a mortgage based on input from two salaries. I had a job I loved as a writer and editor for a congressman from the West Coast.

I had worked my way up from computer operator to chief writer over a period of six years and felt a strong sense of identity and accomplishment in my position. Bruce was not as fulfilled in his job, but he had worked for his congressman for seven years and had no plans to move on.

Our life was exciting—full of fast-paced city life, interesting friends, and togetherness. Since our offices were located in neighboring buildings, we drove to work together in the morning and home again late at night. We had lunch together nearly every day, often picnicking on the scenic lawn of the Capitol's west side, and sometimes rendezvoused at the Coke machines in the underground tunnels connecting the Capitol to the three House office buildings.

Then our boat got rocked.

I now recognize that God's grace went into operation the moment Bruce told me the news. I was just a new Christian, or perhaps I should say "renewed." I had become a Christian as a teenager but abandoned my faith throughout most of my early years and into my mid-twenties. God never let me go, however, and I recommitted my life to Him shortly after I met Bruce. I was twenty-seven when we married; he was twenty-nine. Although I had quite a store of Bible knowledge, I had a lot to learn about how the Lord operates in the lives of those who call on His name.

The first thing God impressed on me was that the job crisis was not a case of bad timing, as it seemed to so many of our friends. I began to sense it was *good timing*. Yes, we had just gotten married. Yes, we had just bought a house. *But it's good that this happened to Bruce after you married him and not before,* I heard God say.

However one looked at it, being "encouraged to move on" felt a lot like being fired. And, right or wrong, working people tend to derive much of their identity and self-worth from their jobs. This had been Bruce's first real job out of college. He had put his whole heart into it and had worked hard to rise from an entry-level position in the hometown office to top legislative assistant in Washington, D.C. It was all he knew, and the change was going to be traumatic. But he had a wife now—me. The Lord made it plain to me that, as his wife, I was to encourage Bruce throughout the difficult process.

God must be in this, I thought, because my immediate reaction was *not* to panic. Sure, our life— my life—was being threatened. The Washington metropolitan area has one of the highest standards of living in the country. We could not afford many weeks on my salary alone, and finding a new job for Bruce was going to be tricky. It would take time— lots of hard-working, pavement-pounding, telephone-networking time.

But somehow I felt at peace. With God's grace, I maintained that peace throughout the next several weeks. That, perhaps more than anything else, was an encouragement to Bruce. If *I* didn't think the world was ending, maybe everything wasn't as bad as it seemed.

We began immediately to pray for God's guidance. We both knew in our *heads* that God's hand was in the situation, but it was especially difficult for Bruce to know it in his *heart*—after all, he was in the thick of the turmoil.

Why had this happened after so many years of faithful service? Bruce wanted to know. *Whose fault was it? Why was he the one to be let go and not someone else?*

Since I had less understanding than Bruce did of his office's operation and political infighting, a large part of me wanted to help him finger the responsible person and hold him down while Bruce tarred and feathered him. But after a time of honest self-evaluation I knew my role as encourager was to turn Bruce's thoughts away from the nonproductive questions of *why?* and *what if?* and focus on *now what?*

Consciously biting my tongue, I listened as he expressed his frustration, anger, and confusion over the next several weeks. I always tried to keep from joining in; rather I hung onto the belief that if God was truly in charge of our lives, then the people who seemed to have control over Bruce were not really making autonomous decisions. They were unwittingly playing a part in a larger plan God had for Bruce—and for me. Again and again I tried to encourage Bruce that God was in charge—not man or circumstances.

Since I had a talent for writing and had studied the fine art of résumé presentation at one time, I helped Bruce prepare a top-notch résumé, pointing out the many skills and talents he had developed in his years in the congressional office—many of which were not necessarily implied in his job title or listed in his job description.

The résumé was encouraging to Bruce. Reading over it, he saw that he had a lot to offer another congressional office or government-related agency or firm. I helped him print it and fashion a cover letter. We sent the résumé to numerous offices on Capitol Hill. We also obtained a list of Washington-based lobbying organizations and targeted about two hundred of them. Then we waited.

Bruce continued to work in his office, although his position as "lame duck" made things extremely uncomfortable. Every day was a reminder that he was in a place where he was no longer needed. He considered just quitting, but we needed the money. He decided to hang in there for as long as he could or until another job opened up.

I was determined to give him all the appreciation and encouragement he was not getting at work. Obviously, the hours in the office seemed interminable to him, so I called him several times through the day just to say "I love you." We rendezvoused for that bottomless can of Coke two or three times a day. It seemed best to stop talking about my own job, since I was happy and fulfilled in it and was even being considered for a promotion. I told him frequently what a terrific husband he was and what a great catch he'd be for another office. We arranged fun things to do with our friends in the city—walks through museums, dinners in Georgetown, sledding near the Pentagon, touch football on the Mall. At home we built cozy fires in our new fireplace and made love often.

There were still times when Bruce would drag through a day and come home upset and depressed—and there seemed to be nothing I could say or do to help. Then I just prayed. Sometimes I, too, felt tired or depressed. But God always seemed to lift us out of the doldrums within a day or two by giving one or both of us a fresh word that He was in charge. *We* weren't even in charge—thank goodness. He was, and He had a plan that was being worked out before our very eyes.

Weeks passed with few bites from the dozens of résumés we had sent out. That was disheartening. Remembering sermons I'd heard and Bible verses I'd studied, I tried to help Bruce consider that every negative response or non-response was God's way of closing a door we shouldn't be going through anyway.

A few congressional offices and some lobbying firms did call. We weeded out those that were not offering a salary and position at least equal to the one Bruce currently had. He went on a number of interviews—none of which excited him. It was hard to turn down legitimate job offers. With the deadline running out on his congressional job and little savings in the bank, it was sometimes all I could do to keep from shouting: "Take it! It's better than nothing!" But we both believed God wanted Bruce's new job to be a positive career move. As his chief encourager I felt it was my duty to keep him from underestimating or undervaluing his services. I didn't want him to sell himself short just to assuage my threatened sense of financial security.

One job opening did seem exciting and well-suited to Bruce's talents and career goals. It was with a lobbying firm involved in an industry that interested Bruce. He went for the initial interview. They liked him and invited him back. He went for a second interview—and made the second cut. The field for the position narrowed to three people, and Bruce was one of them. A last set of interviews stood as the only remaining hurdle.

By this time Bruce felt he had exhausted all of his resources in Washington, D.C. He had tried every avenue he knew to find a good job, and this was the only street that hadn't come up with a red light—yet.

A new thought sparked in my mind: *Perhaps God is saying it's time to leave Washington.* I could hardly believe I was thinking it. I had grown up in the Maryland suburbs of the Washington metropolitan area. All my family—a close-knit network of parents, siblings, aunts, uncles, cousins, grandparents—lived there. I was a family person and a city girl. I loved my job. I fully expected to stay in Washington forever.

But just a few weeks earlier I had begun listening to the tape-recorded services of Bruce's home church in Melbourne, Florida, where his father was pastor. I often found myself singing the songs, remembering names that were mentioned, even praying for the things the congregation prayed for. I was drawn to the lively worship, the anointed preaching, the open-arms spirit that came to life even on tape. One day, as I listened to the people singing, I had a sudden urge to be there in Melbourne with them. I couldn't quite identify the emotion I was experiencing. Incredibly, it seemed I was feeling *homesick*. I could hardly believe the cry I was hearing from my spirit: *I want to go home.*

One night as we made our way through the bumper-to-bumper traffic of North Capitol Street, Bruce surprised me with a question: "How would you feel about moving to Florida if this lobbying job doesn't pan out?"

He knew how I felt about Washington, my job, my family. I think I surprised him even more with my answer: "It would be exciting! Let's talk about it."

We decided to throw out a fleece. If God wanted us to stay in Washington, then Bruce would get the job with the lobbying firm. If we were meant to go to Florida, then he would be turned down. Suddenly a great pressure seemed to be lifted from Bruce's shoulders. My willingness to move with him—and not only willingness, but excitement—was a big boost. He could get the job or not get the job, and everything would be OK. In fact, either way it would be great.

Bruce did not get the Washington job. However, within two weeks of job-hunting in Florida he was offered a challenging position that was right up his alley: public information officer at Kennedy Space Center, covering the activities of NASA's space shuttle program. God had thrown the door wide open, and we walked through it—with no looking back.

We moved to Melbourne, built a house, and quickly became active in the church that had become my spiritual home even before it was my physical home. Today, more than a decade later, we have two children, Scott, eleven, and Kimberly, nine. All of Bruce's rather large family live close by—a loving network of parents, siblings, aunts, uncles, cousins, grandparents. My own parents eventually moved to Melbourne, and several other members of my family now live in Florida as well. In addition to being a mother, I have an exciting job working at home as the associate editor of *Charisma* and *Ministries Today* magazines.

I continue in my role as chief encourager to my husband. I believe this is one of the most significant ministries God has given me as a wife. After all, He thinks Bruce is terrific. He sent His Son to die for him—and to live through him. My job—and my desire—is simply to agree with the Lord about Bruce and be the instrument through which God's love, support, and encouragement can flow. ♥

Michele Buckingham is a wife, mother of two, and associate editor of *Charisma* and *Ministries Today* magazines. Her husband, Bruce, a spokesperson for NASA at the Kennedy Space Center, is the oldest son of the late pastor and author Jamie Buckingham, with whom Michele worked closely for six years. Bruce, Michele, and the kids live in rural Palm Bay, Florida.

12

Minister Peace to Each Other

by Joyce Meyer

J ESUS WAS REFERRED to as the Prince of Peace (Isa. 9:6). As the anointed Prince of Peace, Jesus is a model to show us how the anointing and peace work together.

In the tenth chapter of Luke, Jesus sent seventy men out into the neighboring towns where He was going to visit. He told them to heal the sick and tell the people that the kingdom of God had come close to them. He instructed them to find a house and say, "Peace be to this household!"

If peace settled there and remained, they could remain. If not, they were to move on to another town.

Now after this the Lord chose and appointed seventy others and sent them out ahead of Him, two by two, into every town and place where He Himself was about to come (visit). And He said to them, The harvest indeed is abundant (there is much ripe grain), but the farmhands are few. Pray therefore the Lord of the harvest to send out laborers into His harvest. Go your way; behold, I send you out like lambs into the midst of wolves.

Carry no purse, no provisions bag, no [change of] sandals; refrain from [retarding your journey by] saluting and wishing anyone well along the way. Whatever house you enter, first say, Peace be to this household!—[that is,] freedom from all the distresses that result from sin be with this family. And if anyone [worthy] of peace and blessedness is there, the peace and blessedness you wish shall come upon him; but if not, it shall come back to you. And stay on in the same house, eating and drinking what they provide, for the laborer is worthy of his wages. Do not keep moving from house to house.

—LUKE 10:1–7, AMP

Several years ago I felt led to teach on the subject of peace. I spent an entire day sitting in the middle of my bed studying. I felt as if I were looking for something concerning the subject of peace, and yet I did not know what it was. I searched the Scriptures, waiting for the light of revelation to come to me. Finally, I saw something in Luke 10 that I had never seen previously. I felt the Lord was showing me that peace and power go together. The disciples were sent out to heal the sick and proclaim the kingdom of God. One of their instructions was to find a peaceful place to reside and stay there. I felt the Holy Spirit saying to me, "Joyce, if you want to have a powerful ministry that will help multitudes, find peace and stay in it."

At that time I was not very peaceful. I still had a lot of inner turmoil, and I still caused a lot of upset. I had not yet learned the importance of strife-free living. The Spirit showed me that just as He told the disciples to find a peaceful place and let that be their base of operation, I was to be His house—His base of operation—and He wanted the house He was working in to be peaceful.

I wanted to minister under a strong anointing, and I prayed about it regularly. God was answering my prayer by showing me what I needed to do to enable the anointing to flow.

The believer has God's anointing within. The person called by God to a ministry has the anointing resident in him to do what God has called him to. But sometimes there are things in the believer's life that must be moved out of the way in order to allow the anointing to flow.

I began to notice how the devil would often attempt to stir up strife between Dave and me just before a seminar where we would be ministering. I started to see a pattern.

I also realized why our family had experienced such strong attacks from Satan on Sunday mornings for so many years. The Bible teaches us that the seed of God's Word must be sown in a heart of peace by someone who works for and makes peace.

> And the harvest of righteousness (of confor-
> mity to God's will in thought and deed) is [the
> fruit of the seed] sown in peace by those who
> work for and make peace—in themselves and
> in others, [that is,] that peace which means
> concord (agreement, harmony) between indi-
> viduals, with undisturbedness, in a peaceful
> mind free from fears and agitating passions
> and moral conflicts.
>
> —JAMES 3:18, AMP

Careful examination of this scripture sheds light on the reason the devil attempts to upset people just before they are going to hear the Word of God and have an opportunity to advance in their walk with Him. The enemy also comes immediately after the seed is sown, hoping to steal the Word.

> The sower sows the Word. The ones along the
> path are those who have the Word sown [in
> their hearts], but when they hear, Satan comes
> as once and (by force) takes away the message
> which is sown in them.
>
> —MARK 4:14–15, AMP

Satan is intent on stealing the Word before it takes root in you. He knows if it takes root in your heart that it will begin to produce good fruit. We must operate in the wisdom of God from within and show ourselves wiser than the enemy. We cannot sit by passively and allow him to get us so upset before we get to church that we cannot hear or retain what is being said. Nor can we allow him to get us upset after we leave. It's important for us to be able to think about the Word that has been preached and taught to us.

> And He said to them, Be careful what you are hearing. The measure [of thought and study] you give [to the truth you hear] will be the measure [of virtue and knowledge] that comes back to you, and more [besides] will be given to you who hear.
>
> —MARK 4:24, AMP

Satan will often attack your mind after hearing the Word lest you begin to meditate on it. I can remember our family arguing all the way to church on Sunday mornings, but living in pretense that all was well as soon as we saw anyone we knew. I would "fake" my way through the service, clapping at all the right places, saying "Amen!" at the appropriate times and pretend to pay attention to the pastor while he preached. All the while, I was planning how I would ignore Dave or the kids until they apologized to me. I certainly did not intend to go home and fix them a nice dinner. I really did not even plan to talk to them. Satan delighted in those "flesh" days.

I was deceived. I did not understand what was going on. Everything would be fine one minute, and the next thing I knew, everyone would be mad—screaming and yelling. Or, to the other extreme, everyone would be deathly quiet—so cold and quiet that it was obvious feelings were hurt and wrong thoughts were running rampant. Strife is bickering, arguing, heated disagreement, and an angry undercurrent. We definitely had strife, and I believe a lot of other families and individuals do also.

Choose to Be a Peacemaker

EVEN NORMAL NOISE can be upsetting to a person who has a lot on his mind. Just before one of our services, I am busy meditating on what God has given me to minister that day. I do not hide from my family, but I have asked them to refrain from telling me anything right before a meeting that would tend to be upsetting. They help me by trying to keep the atmosphere peaceful. You can also help your loved ones by maintaining peace, especially when you know they are already under pressure.

When a husband comes home from an especially trying day at the office, his wife can minister peace to him by directing the children into an activity that creates a calmer atmosphere, rather than a chaotic one.

When the wife has been cleaning and cooking all day for a special holiday family get-together the next day, the husband can minister peace to her by taking the children somewhere for the evening and allowing her to have a nice long block of quiet time.

If a child has been taking final exams for a week and is already under stress, the parents might choose to withhold correction until the stress of the exams has ended for his messy room or for leaving his bike out on the driveway.

We can help each other to avoid strife by being a little more sensitive to one another's needs. Sow good seeds, and you will reap a good harvest in your own time of need. After being married to Dave for more than thirty years, I can tell when he is tired or not feeling good. I have learned to minister peace to him at those times, instead of bringing up a problem to him right then.

He is a very peaceful man and would probably handle himself quite well even if I did bring up a problem, but there is no point in adding weight to an already heavy load. The devil likes to place heavy loads on us that are hard to bear and then keeps pressing until we blow. But the Word of God teaches us to watch out for one another. This is part of the love walk.

> Strive to live in peace with everybody, and pursue that consecration and holiness without which no one will [ever] see the Lord. Exercise foresight and be on the watch to look [after one another], to see that no one falls back from and fails to secure God's grace.
> —HEBREWS 12:14–15, AMP

Grace is unmerited favor. We can simply do someone a favor and help him by not placing undue pressure upon him during tedious times. For me, it is when I am getting ready to minister. Satan is looking for any crack to crawl through. For you it may be some other area, but we all have them. He seeks to get us in strife so the anointing cannot flow.

There is an anointing for everything that we are called to do—not just for spiritual things. People laugh when I say this, but there is an anointing that comes on me to shop. If it's there, the trip is very fruitful and enjoyable. If it's not, I cannot find anything I am looking for. I can't seem to make decisions about what to buy. Even if I find something I like, I don't seem to have any real desire to buy it. I say in times like that, "If I buy anything today, it will have to jump off the rack and just get on my body."

One evening recently, Dave and I went shopping. We stopped to get a sandwich and were intending to spend the evening together at the mall. I needed to get a birthday present for our daughter and just wanted to look around. Dave usually enjoys that, but this particular evening he became extremely tired about thirty minutes after we got there.

I was just getting into my shopping, when he started rushing and hurrying me to get something so we could go. I felt hurt and offended. I could feel the strife come in immediately and the anointing disappear. All of a sudden, I wanted to leave. I was not feeling peaceful.

I had been working hard and had not spent as much personal time with Dave as I like to. I was really looking forward to having the evening with him, and when he acted as if he did not want to be there, I immediately had to start fighting anger, unforgiveness, strife, negative thoughts, and tears.

I knew it was an attack, but that did not make it any less real. Dave knew I was having a hard time controlling my emotions, so he stayed very quiet. We left the parking lot and started home. We had just gotten on the highway when we came within an inch of having a car accident. If we had not been spared by what I believe were God's angels, we would have been hit on both sides at once.

What started out to be a lovely evening had suddenly turned into a chaotic mess of upset and strife. This is just the way the spirit of strife operates. It tries to catch you off guard, or at a time when you're tired and more likely to give in rather than resist it.

Dave told me later that it was unbelievable how badly he felt and how quickly it came on him. He had been fine when we arrived at the mall, and suddenly he felt he could not stand to stay.

You might think it sounds a bit out of balance to talk of being anointed for such things as shopping, cleaning house, or other ordinary chores. However, I firmly believe that God's Spirit is available to help us do anything that is the Lord's will and that's in His timing.

There is another revelation in the second verse of Psalm 133. When the priests were anointed, the oil was first poured on their head. Then it ran down on the collar and skirt of their garments. God called my attention to this principle: *The anointing flows down from the head.*

My husband is anointed to lead our family. If I am in strife with him, the anointing that is upon him will not flow down to me, and I will begin to sense struggle in our relationship. It can effect other family matters that could be handled with ease if I stay under his covering.

There is an anointing that rests on the head or the leader of a company, even if you don't like him or agree with him. When an individual is in strife with the head (open or underlying), the anointing cannot flow down to that person, and his job will be a struggle. He will dread going to work. He may even make foolish mistakes. Although he knows he is qualified to do the work, for some reason he keeps making errors.

This is a life principle. God has designed leadership to preserve order. God called Moses and anointed Aaron to help him. When the job became too much for them, God allowed Moses to anoint others to head up smaller groups of people. Each group had a captain, and even the captains had a leader. It's God's way, even if we don't like it.

Protect the anointing on your life by keeping the strife out. Live by the anointing. God has given it to you to help you in all that you do. Things are not accomplished by might nor power, but by His Spirit (Zech. 4:6). Stay peaceful and calm; be quick to forgive, slow to anger, patient, and kind. ♥

Joyce Meyer is an internationally recognized minister and author of more than fifteen books, including the bestsellers *Beauty for Ashes* and *The Root of Rejection*. Joyce is the founder of Life In The Word ministry, and she broadcasts *Life In The Word* radio and television programs on hundreds of stations nationwide.

Material in this chapter was taken from *Life Without Strife* (Creation House).

Part Three

Fulfill His Dreams

13

Get Yourself a Black Negligee

by Betty Malz

ALL WOMEN ARE not *created* equal, but we do have equal opportunity for improvement. Life is not fair. There are many inequalities in life. Look around you.

A counselor told me about a call he received from a married man: "Please pray that God will take this angel home to glory and give me a flesh-and-blood woman who will cook, love me, and take care of the kids. My wife knows where every retreat is being held, sings in a trio with Mollie Missionary, Sainted Sally, and Dolly Do Good, but she can't find the kitchen and has forgotten where the bedroom is."

The counselor paid them an unexpected visit at midday the following Saturday. He found the man propped up on the couch wearing a sweaty under-shirt, watching football, drinking a can of beer, burping, and scratching . . . Across the room with a cat on her lap sat a fairly young wife in a faded, pink chenille bathrobe.

We have equal opportunities for improvement.

Our family had just celebrated Christmas. I was given a couple of gifts that were not wrapped but were still appreciated. However, I was most fasci-nated by a package that was tied with a red lace bow over a green porcelain-finish paper. Wrapping makes a statement. It says, *I care about you. You may be a practical package, but you need to guard against the infamous "eight-year plateau." Go out and buy yourself a black lace negligee, for him.*

At a retreat in Texas a man told me, "If you wanna know if a man is happy, slip into his home when everyone is away. Check to see if the kitchen is used and if there is a black lace nightie in her drawer."

During the holidays our church had a banquet. After the meal the special entertainment was a bridal parade of all the women who could still get into their wedding gowns. As I was putting mine on, it took two women to hold the sides while a third lady zipped up the back for me. I hadn't worn it for eighteen years, but I'd only gained eight pounds, I reasoned. Still, I almost didn't make it into the parade. I knew I had to get rid of that excess.

You can change.

Lot's wife refused to change. She could have, but she wouldn't—and she turned into a pillar of salt. If your marriage dies, and the light in your husband's eyes goes out, don't let it be your fault. Get his attention and keep it.

Captivating a man is not a new game. Rebecca, another Bible character, means "captivating." She captivated Isaac and was a vital link in the continuation of Abraham's seed. You can be captivating too. Don't let your appearance go.

Sarah means "princess." But the princess got impatient and her husband, Abram, made love to a servant girl named Hagar, which means "wanderer." It is possible for a Christian woman to become a wanderer instead of a princess, but I'm sure it would be more pleasant to live with a princess than a wanderer. Do your best to look and act like a princess.

While writing this chapter I talked at length with a gynecologist. He confirms that interest and participation are different with each couple. Many men immersed in some lengthy project at work refrain from making love until the project is completed—then declare a holiday to catch up. The gynecologist told me his guide rule is that a relatively healthy couple of reasonable age makes love an average of twice a week. If that couple loves less than once a week, they are lazy. "Busy, hard-working couples who make love more than three times a week are crazy." He grinned.

He went on to say, "If you put your heart into your marriage, your body will follow. Work at being intimate, and sex will automatically follow." Sit close to him, touch him, ride in the truck to haul trash with him. Be there for him.

Many a woman will spend three hours in a beauty salon and cook for two hours to prepare a meal but won't spend twenty minutes in the bedroom to satisfy her mate's sexual need.

Wear that black negligee.

95

As a couple grows older, especially if there is a great difference in age, they can work at the facets of a relationship that doesn't wane with time. The doctor left me with an illustration: He talked with a woman of eighty and her husband, who was eighty-two. The man told the doctor they had sex almost every night. Looking at the withered little wife, he asked her, "Is he telling the truth?" She smiled wanly. "Yes, almost every night. We *almost did* Monday night, we *almost did* Tuesday night, we *almost did* Wednesday night. . . . "

Think about it. One intimate rendezvous is more meaningful than frequent, weak quickies without atmosphere. Take the phone off the hook; light a candle; give him your undivided attention. Let him know this is special for you. This short investment of time will be a valid form of insurance for your marriage. ♥

14

Fitness Is Appealing

by Stormie Omartian

WHEN I FINISHED my second book, an emotion-
ally exhausting autobiographical account of my life
as an abused child, I looked in the mirror and did
not like what I saw. "My husband needs a new wife,"
I said to my reflection, "and it's going to be *me!*"

In order to meet the deadline for my book I had
let a few things go concerning my physical self. I
looked old, tired, lifeless, and out of shape. And I
felt just as bad as I looked. Although my husband
never voiced any specific complaints about what he
observed in me, he wasn't especially excited about
it either.

I had long been aware of what steps were

necessary to stay healthy and fit, and I knew which steps I had violated or ignored. So the cause of my depleted state was not a mystery—neither was the solution. I set out to practice what I had preached for many years. Within thirty days I was a new woman, and my husband had a new wife. I noticed an immediate positive response from him with every step I took toward my goal. Let me encourage you to do what I did.

First of all, you need to be convinced that what *is not* appealing to any man is a wife who is listless, sluggish, tired, lifeless, depressed, sickly, bored, undernourished, colorless, tense, drawn, sagging, flabby, and aging rapidly. What *is* appealing is a wife who is energetic, sparkling, positive, youthful, attractive, healthy, colorful, exuberant, and full of vitality. All these appealing qualities come with being fit.

It doesn't matter how old you are, what you weigh, or what your body has been through. There is something you can be doing to raise your fitness level. I know people in their thirties who are old and people in their seventies and eighties who are young. Because there is something special about every age, a woman doesn't have to fear getting older as long as she takes proper care of herself. What you don't want is to become too sickly and decrepit to enjoy any part of your life. You also don't want to appear older than you really are. Premature aging is a sign that the body is out of balance and out of order. A woman should always desire to have a youthful vitality, and that can happen at any age.

You can also be fit no matter what your body size is. I've seen women who carry excess weight still keep their muscles toned, their circulation moving, and their bodies cleansed. They continue to maintain a youthful attractiveness that is very appealing to a husband.

Fitness is to be desired because through it you can have increased stamina to face life's experiences. You can minimize PMS and menopausal symptoms, elevate your mood, shake a depressed feeling, control stress, and generally enjoy better health. Fitness is also of utmost importance for your self-image and confidence. It causes you to feel better about yourself and frees you to focus on your husband's needs. How you think about yourself will always affect how you respond to him. You'll be a much more loving and responsive partner if you're not thinking about how terrible you look or how tired you feel.

There are seven steps to staying youthful, attractive, and fit. These are the steps in the order in which I did them:

The first step was to take stock of my life and to see if there was any stress in it that could be alleviated, or, better yet, eliminated. I took active measures to do just that. Stress is aging and takes your immune system to the point of breakdown if not controlled and offset by diet and exercise. Being consumed with negative attitudes such as unforgiveness, bitterness, hatred, anger, and criticism is very stressful to the body, not to mention unattractive. How much better it is to spend time with God in His Word and in prayer over these matters. Giving praise and thanks to God is one of the best forms of stress control there is. It is the first step toward getting fit in any area of your life.

The next thing I did was to go on a three-day

water fast in order to seek the Lord and cleanse myself spiritually and physically. After the fast I ate only fruit and vegetables for another day or two. Already I felt I had a new lease on life.

The third step was to begin doing some kind of physical exercise every day. I followed my own exercise tape three times a week, and on the off-days I took a brisk walk or went bicycle riding with my children or my husband. Exercise puts a sparkle in your eyes, a glow on your skin, and a youthful spring in your step better than anything I know. It's something other people will notice immediately while you're still measuring your hips to see if they are shrinking. One of the main benefits of exercise is that it flushes poisons and toxic wastes from the body. It also increases circulation, strengthens muscles, and builds your endurance. It is an irreplaceable way to free the body from impurities that lead to premature aging and illness.

The fourth step was to make certain I was drinking sixty-four ounces of pure, fresh water daily. To do that I drank sixteen ounces four times a day: a half-hour before breakfast, lunch, dinner, and bedtime. This flushes the system of poisons and helps every organ in your body function properly.

The fifth step I took was to pay strict attention to what I was eating. I ruthlessly eliminated all junk and strictly ate food the way God made it, or as close to that as possible. I had given up sugar, white flour, all chemicalized, high processed "food-less" foods years ago. But I needed to be careful to eat many more raw or properly cooked fruits and vegetables, plus whole grains, pure meat, and fish.

Step six was to make sure I got out in the fresh

air and sunlight for at least a few minutes every day. We need fresh air, and sunlight for life. Seeing to it that you do not live in a dark hole is important to fitness. Of course, be cautious to wear sunscreen when needed and not allow yourself to have over-exposure to the sun.

The seventh step crucial to fitness was making sure I got plenty of rest. You can only be sure of getting proper, rejuvenating rest if you are getting plenty of healthy food, exercise, pure water, fresh air and sunshine and not living under constant stress. Step seven almost falls into place when the other steps are in proper balance. The reason getting good rest is so critical is that, during sleep, food is transformed into tissue; the cells of your body are repaired and reproduced; and the blood cleanses itself. If you don't allow your body proper rest, these processes can't take place. Health and attractiveness depend on good sleep, and not getting enough can age you quicker than anything else.

Once I started taking steps in these seven areas, noticeable changes happened quickly in my relationship with my husband. The most apparent was his renewed interest in the two of us spending more time together. My new zest for life stirred his interest, and he took steps toward fitness himself. His openness to being included somewhat in my health regimen was a boost to his vitality, and as a result we both had more energy to devote to one another. I found that really loving your husband requires preparation of your spirit, soul, *and* body. One of the ways you express love for your husband is by how you eat, exercise, and take care of yourself. The bottom line is that fitness enhances the quality and length of your existence here on this earth. For a husband, it's always more appealing to have a wife who makes choices for life. ♥

Stormie Omartian is the author of seven books, including *Stormie, The Power of a Praying Parent, The Power of a Praying Wife, Greater Health God's Way,* and *A Step in the Right Direction.* She has five exercise videos, three of which were certified gold, and has written lyrics to hundreds of recorded songs. Stormie lives in Tennessee with her husband, Michael, and their three children: Christopher, age twenty-one; John, age eighteen; and Amanda, age sixteen.

15

Stay Attractive

by Jane Hansen

*I*T'S COLD, *and it's dark. It's fall, and I hate fall. Everything around me is dying, and tonight I feel a part of my life is dying too. Howard is out for the evening, and even though there's a fire in the fireplace it gives me no comfort. I let the cats in for company, but they want only their food and the warm cozy fire. I listen, but there are no longer any sounds in our home since the children are all gone.*

Such were my thoughts one night, all negative. I turned and caught sight of my reflection in the glass patio door. *Was I showing signs of dying too?* My eyes were sinking into the recesses of my face, and those tiny lines now seemed deeper and more apparent. My pale skin was no longer tight, and without the touch of a pencil my eyebrows had ceased to exist. My hair reminded me of a brown felt hat pulled down over my ears if I granted it just a few months without attention. . . .

As I continued my examination below my neck, I found similar flaws. Flaws that were there at birth, ones that went virtually unnoticed in the innocence of my childhood, had steadily become more apparent with age.

The old feeling crept back from my past.

Am I really plain, ordinary, simple, unattractive?

A cold chill ran down my spine, and I pulled my robe tightly around my body. I climbed the stairs to Scott's empty bedroom and opened his closet, in which I now stored our old family pictures. Choosing several boxes, I returned to the fireplace. As I settled down on the floor, my mind brought into focus a snapshot of a small girl sitting slumped at a picnic table. Her eyes were sad. The words of my mother blew like a trumpet in my head: "Plain Jane, a sweet child, but, oh, so ordinary. She'll never be a great beauty."

Those words and that picture colored my life, my beliefs about myself and even how I approached events and people. Somehow I turned those words into a belief that if I could be beautiful and create beautiful surroundings, I would be loved and accepted.

Years ago God showed me this wrong belief, and together we have been working through its control in my life. I opened the boxes and thumbed through the pictures. I remembered different times and saw people who had been a part of my life.

How might these relationships have been different, I wondered, if I hadn't believed I was ugly and needed to be beautiful to be accepted?

As I poured myself a cup of hot tea and let the warm liquid touch my lips, I felt God touch my heart. "But, Jane," He seemed to be saying, "I have shown you this old picture and uncovered your wrong belief in order to set you free."

"Yes, Lord," I said. "You have touched a place of inadequacies deep inside me. You have proven You care about all of me. Yes, even when it is painful You desire only good for me."

The fire grew brighter, and my cats snuggled next to me. Peace and contentment settled over me.

The sound of a car pulling into the driveway shook me from my reverie. Howard hurried inside.

"Is it ever cold and windy out there!" he said as he hung his jacket in the hall closet. Stepping into the living room, he caught sight of all the pictures on the floor. Slowly, without moving his eyes from me, he came closer and reached out his hand to me. Pulling me up from the floor, he said, "Jane, you're beautiful, and you've made our house so inviting. I love you. I am so glad to be home."

He gave unto them beauty for ashes . . .
—Isaiah 61:3, kjv

Is beauty only skin deep? Is beauty only a combination of our outer appearance with adornments to emphasize our best features? Or does real beauty stem from something deep inside, something God puts there, that comes through even the plainest shell? I believe it is a coming together of both—

a deep inner glow of a spirit united with Jesus, and the best choices we can make to enhance our outer physical appearance.

If you come face to face with the Godhead, you would be confronted with beauty in the fullest measure—beauty that touches more than the eyes. It would touch your heart and reach the depths of your emotions. Webster defines *beauty* as "the quality of being very pleasing, as in form, color." God not only is the very essence of beauty, He desires beauty. Following through Scripture, you see how God designed beauty in all He created. In His description of the new Jerusalem, He chose words that cue our minds to visualize a city both great and beautiful.

Therefore God, who is beauty, who desires beauty, who creates beauty, created us in His own image. Man was a beautiful creation with a desire for beauty inherited from his Creator. Not only is it acceptable to desire beauty, but this very desire is an attribute of our Father.

But what God created, sin perverted. The heart and its motives hold the answers to what determines sinful behavior.

Early in my life I formed the belief that if I were beautiful and made my surroundings beautiful, like my mother, then I'd be loved and accepted. While it was never a conscious thought, nevertheless it was what my heart believed, and it drove me to produce what I felt would meet my needs. I believed I was ugly, but if I could make myself attractive I would feel loved.

I have always had an innate desire to be surrounded by beauty. My mother was a beautiful woman who created, from nothing, a place of beauty in herself and in our home, and more times than not the house provided for the pastor—my father—was old and needed a lot of work.

I remember one such house where the kitchen was dark and dreary with only one small window for light. We had barely moved in before Mother was saying, "Come on now, Jane—here is a paint-brush for you. Let's paint this kitchen all white." My job was to paint the floor. Soon that dark kitchen became white from floor to ceiling. After she moved our table and chairs in, she set up her sewing machine and once again went to work to transform the sterile white kitchen into a place of beauty. "Here, Jane, tie this cushion on the last chair, and then we'll be finished. See what you can do with just a little imagination and a lot of work!"

Hung at the window were bright red ruffled curtains, and matching placemats lay on the table. Mother warmed the room with candlelight, added fresh flowers, and soon it was as inviting as an Irish stew on a cold winter's evening. Once she added the scent of freshly baked bread, you never wanted to leave her kitchen. She kept a sense of order in our home, so simple and yet homey and cozy. She provided her family with stability.

Mother dressed modestly, as befitted a pastor's wife, but she always presented herself well put-together. She brought me up to follow her routine. I can still hear myself saying, "Ninety-eight, ninety-nine, one hundred! OK, Mommy, I've had my bath, powdered myself, brushed my teeth, and brushed my hair one hundred strokes."

"Oh, Jane, what a good little girl you are. If you

keep working as you do now, one day you'll grow up to be just like me." Thus I grew up with a role model who created an environment that validated my own desire for beauty.

By the time I met Howard I was working daily to keep a sense of beauty and grace about myself. I saw marriage as the answer to my deepest need, the avenue to fulfilling all my desires.

Howard was busy pursuing his career, and I was busy pursuing mine. As a wife I was there for Howard, but with a motive of ultimately getting love and acceptance for myself. I liked entertaining and creating a memorable evening for our guests and his clients. I worked hard at creating a home where he could unwind and relax. As a mother I applied my energies to training my children to become responsible adults. Everything I ever dreamed possible was happening in my life.

I was drawing my self-worth from what I could create. Who I was, how I was loved and accepted, soon depended on how well I kept up not only my appearance but my home, my children, my table, my car—and, yes, even the dog. It was now my full-time job to create a wife, a home, and a family to gain my husband's love and acceptance.

Like me, Howard brought inadequacies and fears into our marriage. They soon caused him to pull away from me on all levels except the barest essentials.

I floundered. What was wrong with me? Why could I no longer create what Howard needed? Was I no longer attractive? Was our home no longer a place of peace and rest for Howard? What had I done?

My self-worth, which I had learned to base on my

successful performance, plummeted to the depths of depression. I wandered through life from day to day, performing the best I knew how but with no results. Days turned into years, and my questions turned into a desperate search that drew me closer and closer to God.

As the years passed, the hurt inside me had changed to anger I was no longer able to control. I felt like a kettle of boiling water with the lid jumping and hot liquid spewing out, scalding whatever it touched. I could no longer keep the lid on my anger.

One particularly hot evening I slammed the window shut so no one could hear my cries. It had happened again: Howard's silence was more than I could bear. "Dear God!" I screamed. "When is the pain going to end?" My hand ached. I had slammed it down on the table just before I ran out of the room. "I can't stand it anymore!" I jumped up and ran back to the kitchen where Howard was finishing his dinner. Then I lit into him once more.

"What is wrong with me? Say something. Say anything!" I shouted.

His silence grew louder. My carefully kept exterior was coming apart, and it was ugly. The dam had broken, and nothing could keep the floodwaters back. What did God want? Just what did He expect?

In desperation, I sought help from our pastor. He suggested Howard and I begin to meet with him and his wife to sort out our behavior and look at our motives.

Over the next two years God opened up my wrong beliefs and attitudes. First to surface was my perverted desire to create beauty to gain love and acceptance. God showed me I was a worthwhile person simply because I was His child, and His love for me didn't depend on how well I could perform. Slowly, understanding dropped from my head to my heart. Anger was dispelled, and peace flowed back into my world. I was set free from the need to control.

No matter what I did, I could never meet Howard's needs, nor could he meet mine. That was a place for God, and only God. To have anyone or anything other than God in that place was spiritual adultery.

As I saw my tremendous error, confessed it, and repented, I was set free to pursue my desire for beauty with a pure motive: to experience it as an inherent trait from my heavenly Father rather than a sinful need for love and acceptance.

Howard has reaped the overflow from my open relationship with God. As I look to God to meet my needs instead of to Howard, it releases him to love me without my expectations pressuring him to give me security. We are both experiencing a new freedom to be who we really are and to love one another without seeking for ourselves.

If you desire beauty, pursue it; enjoy it; create it with your Father's blessing. But ask God to examine your motives and see if the Holy Spirit needs to adjust your heart. He gave me beauty for ashes. He will do the same for you. ♥

Jane Hansen serves as international president of Aglow International, logging more than 100,000 miles annually throughout the United States and abroad to share a message of God's unique call to women in this significant decade. Her desire is for God's healing and restoration to reach into women's lives in order that they may embrace all God wills to do through them in the body of Christ.

Her book, *Fashioned for Intimacy, Reconciling Men and Women to God's Original Design* (Regal Books), helps people to understand God's plan to reconcile the relationship between men and women.

An ordained minister, Jane Hansen serves in leadership roles with organizations that represent the body of Christ, including the Spiritual Warfare Network and the International Charismatic Consultation of World Evangelization Advisory Council. She also serves on the advisory board for the Regent University School of Divinity, the International Reconciliation Coalition International Board, and the March for Jesus USA National Advisory Board.

Jane's husband, Howard is a travel industry specialist. They have three married children and several grandchildren.

16

The Beauty of Holiness

by Devi Titus

W OMEN OFTEN misunderstand holiness. They attach religious trappings to themselves in an effort to be spiritual, evident sometimes by their appearance, but more often by their "Christianized" language.

For example, the same lady who "has a word" is habitually late and undependable. Another, who details her recent fast during her testimony, is independent, rebellious, and unsubmitted. If we tune our ears into a women's group, it will not be uncommon to hear phrases such as "the Lord said," "while praying," "during prayer," and so forth. This type of language does not make us more holy. It merely offers a cover-up to what is often the true state of our spirituality. Jesus forbade us to display our prayer practices and instructed us to pray in secret. Nor did He want us to boast of fasting. Such actions do not exemplify the beauty of holiness.

Beauty is an image most women strive for. We can spend endless hours and countless dollars grooming our hair, using fine cosmetics, manicuring our nails and buying our clothing. In fact, I greatly enjoy every aspect of all these procedures. My husband enjoys the results. Among the five basic needs of a husband listed in *His Needs, Her Needs* (Revell) by Willard Harley Jr. is a man's need to have an attractive wife. But we must remember that beauty without holiness is like a flower without color or a sentence without a verb. It is the verb that is the link between the subject of our sentence and the object; thus holiness gives substance to our beauty and direction for our purpose.

While adornment of our appearance is important to our husband, so is the adornment of our spirit. There are two biblical adornments we must put equal effort into: a meek spirit and a quiet spirit. Extrovert personality that I am, always with an opinion, I actually thought I needed to become timid and quiet in order to fulfill these spiritual qualities. I prayed, I tried hard, but I could never succeed at being too quiet for any length of time. Now I understand that meekness is the character quality that keeps us from being provoked easily by others, and a quiet spirit is the quality that keeps me from provoking others easily. I can acquire both and still be the expressive person that God made me to be. Just imagine how fewer fights a marriage would have if the wife spent as much time adorning her spirit as her body!

Holiness is not religious practices; it is the development of godliness within the inner core of a person. The most wonderful gift a wife can give to her husband is to be a lady of fine character, because in holiness or godly character lie purity and trust, two attributes that a marriage relationship must possess.

When Jesus said, "Blessed are the pure in heart, for they shall see God," He did not mean the sinless, unstained, perfect one, but rather the sincere one. Sincerity is merely motivated eagerness to do what is right. The word *sincerity* comes from two Latin words, *sine,* meaning "without," and *cere,* meaning "wax." When Romans tried to copy the craftsmanship of Greek pottery, they often used inferior materials. Therefore, they filled small cracks or pock marks with wax and painted over them. Putting the vessel under fire, the unsuspecting buyer discovered the wax. Quality pottery thus carried the label "sine cere."

To pay more attention to outer beauty than inner character is like putting wax on our flaws and then painting over the flawed product to appear as someone we are not. This, of course, leads us to deceit, trying to live up to something that is only a simulation of what we really are. Merely covering up our defects causes us to sidestep the issue of dealing with our inner character flaws. This lack of sincerity will slowly eat away the trust in a marriage relationship.

Our son, Aaron, was selected by his peers to give the National Honor Society speech on character to the entire student body at his public high school. He opened his speech like this:

"People can rob you of your reputation but not your character; they can steal your image but not your substance; because character, your moral foundation, is not *who* you are but *what* you are. In times of adversity, pain, or emotional suffering, the person with weak character will fall. A biblical parable tells of two men who built houses. One built his house on rock while the other built his house on sand. When the rains, the winds, and the floods beat on the houses, the one built on rock remained, but the one built on sand was destroyed. Thus the life built on good character will withstand hardship, and the life built on poor character will succumb to hardship."

Holiness is beautiful in itself. It projects a clarity in a person's countenance like nothing else and is often reflected through our eyes. One man said that a woman's eyes are the singular most attractive part of her person when he desires a relationship. The eyes become the tangible bridge between our inner beauty and our outer beauty. The eyes are an entrance to the soul. When a couple begins having problems, they cease looking into one another's eyes and begin looking at one another's face. When their lives become clouded by the effects of sin, and their hearts are not pure, the sparkle in their eyes disappears.

Ringing through my memory in the tune of my mother's voice is an old adage: "Beauty is as beauty does." I would like to go a step further by saying, "Beauty does and beauty thinks." The condition of one's soul, that which determines the clearness of one's eyes or the brilliance of one's countenance, becomes the result of one's thoughts.

The answer to the question "Who may ascend to the hill of the Lord?" in Psalm 24:3–4 is, "He who has clean hands and a pure heart, who has not lifted up his soul to falsehood, and has not sworn deceitfully." All four attributes are character qualities. Clean hands are descriptive of one who is innocent in his actions. Actions, or behavioral patterns, are an outcome of a person's heart. However, one does not have a pure heart without having a clean mind.

Keeping your mind clean is ridding your mind of negativity. Your thought life gives direction to your reactions. Consequently, if one wants positive actions, one must have positive thoughts. "Whatever is true . . . honorable . . . right . . . pure . . . lovely . . . of good repute, if there is any excellence and if anything worthy of praise, let your mind dwell on these things" (Phil. 4:8).

The beauty of your marriage relationship will be enhanced by fixing your mind on something worthy of edification rather than on the uncompleted task of your mate. It is here that the ascension process begins. You will rise above the petty disappointments in life and will dwell in the beauty of praise—truly a holy place.

Holiness, like character, does not have an apex. One never attains all that holiness is, for it can always be improved. As time passes our physical beauty fades. Holiness, however, has no pull of gravity nor limitation of age but only increases with time as our devotion to God grows. The beauty of holiness is unfading.

To really love your husband, like loving the Lord, is to love him with the beauty of holiness. ♥

Devi Titus is the wife of Larry Titus, pastor of Fifth Avenue Community Church in Youngstown, Ohio, and serves as administrative pastor of their church. They are the parents of two adult children and two grandchildren. Devi founded *Virtue* magazine, is on the advisory board for *Ministries Today,* and the advisory board and writing staff for *Excellence* magazine. She is a national women's conference speaker and has developed the seminar series, "Ten Smart Choices a Woman Can Make to Improve Her Life." To meet Devi is to "experience Devi" one woman once said. "She says what others think." The life of Devi Titus has impacted masses of women in this generation.

17

Having Fun Together

by Carolyn Jones

W HILE REMINISCING of fun times spent with my husband over these thirty-one years of marriage, I raced off in twenty different directions. I remembered the early days: John in law school while I taught first grade; no money to do things with; playing monopoly and bridge; serving hot dogs and baked beans to dinner guests. My thoughts bounced from that extreme to the other: elaborate family vacations; ski trips; visits to other parts of the country. Then I thought about the simple pleasures: trips to the beach, dinner out.

The more I pondered the more confused I became. What about the not-so-fun times, the tough places, moments out of harmony? And slowly the dawn began to break. The fun times never depended ultimately on what we did, but the attitude of our hearts! That was why pinching pennies in law school was as much fun as fancy vacations.

Paul says in Philippians 4:11–12, "I have learned in whatever state I am to be content: I know how to be abased and I know how to abound. Everywhere and in all things I have learned both to be full and to be hungry, both to abound and to suffer need" (NKJV).

Well, Paul, that's wonderful, but how do we learn that? Knowing it's the attitude of the heart isn't quite the same as putting it into practice. How do we learn to have fun together? If it's not dependent on how much money we have or where we live or how we do things, then how do we develop contentment, fun, enjoyable moments?

God gave me a big key long ago. It's so simple— such a little word—and yet so easily forgotten. It's something we all love to do, never do enough, and need to do more. When all else fails, *laugh!*

You know God must have a sense of humor—look how crazy we are sometimes. Proverbs 17:22 (KJV) says, "A merry heart doeth good like a medicine." Learning to laugh is easier when we understand each other and the reasons we're so different. What a challenge it is when God takes two different sexes, two different backgrounds, and two different temperaments and puts them together! Let's take a look at some specifics.

Understanding the differences in your temperaments really helps alleviate conflict. I am married to a sanguine—a fun-loving, cheerful, people-oriented man who loves nothing more than to help and be involved with people. I've always been attracted to John's loving, giving nature. I was shy inside when John and I met, trying to prove to the world I was "somebody." For John it seemed so easy. He just naturally loved everybody, and God in His infinite wisdom gave me not only what I needed but what I needed to make me grow! Here I was, a melancholy, organized, on-schedule person, and I had married a man who lets organization or being on time take a definite back seat when someone—anyone—needs him! Did I just waltz into this laughing? No!

I remember a Christmas concert at our church several years ago. To get a seat at these popular concerts you have to stand in a long line that winds all the way around the building. To save time (because John was running late) he let me off to stand in line while he parked the car. Twenty minutes later I saw John working his way down the line. He was having a wonderful time. He knew most of the people and was meeting the ones he didn't—a whole line full of people to talk to!

Those of you who have a melancholy, introspective, mull-it-over temperament can readily imagine my reaction. I began to feel sorry for "poor me." *Why,* I asked myself, *do I always have to do the work, hold the place in line, put the children in the church nursery? John has all the fun, and I do all the mundane tasks.*

My pity party was gaining momentum. I popped several martyr pills as I reminded myself of all the times I did the dirty work.

Finally John reached our place in line. He was glowing. To him this was better than the concert, but I was ready. I was so logical. "John," I began, "why is it that I always do the work, hold the place in line and all that, and you have all the fun? You've enjoyed every single person in line, and here I stand alone."

I can still remember the look of absolute shock on John's face. "Oh, Carolyn," he replied, "I'm so sorry. I had no idea!" And without hesitating one second he tapped the shoulder of the person in front of me and said, "Excuse me, sir. My wife would like to talk to you." Mortified, embarrassed, and put in my place, I stammered out something while my sweet husband smiled attentively, knowing he had "solved my problem."

We have a choice: laugh or stew. It's easier to laugh, though, when we understand the differences in what makes each of us tick.

Learning to enjoy the differences instead of grinding our teeth can go a long way in our marriages.

I hate to be late, but I'm married to a man who can be standing in front of the mirror shaving, still in his undershorts, and saying, "I'm ready." Several years ago in my logical, time-oriented way I said, "John, you're still not dressed. We're late, and you were supposed to get the babysitter at 6:30." John glanced at the clock that said 6:55 and said, "Don't worry, Carolyn—I'll make it." He really meant it! No problem to a sanguine.

Might as well laugh—consider the alternative. Just think how awful it would be if I'd married someone just like me! Well, I'd be on time, but I'd probably also be a nervous wreck.

I'm learning. One Valentine's Day John came rushing in the door at dinner time. Seeing the present I had wrapped for him, he grabbed it up and asked, "Oh, can I open this now?" I was a little surprised at his eagerness but said that he could. John unwrapped the gift hurriedly, barely taking notice of what it was, and went down the hall to the study. Why was he in such a hurry to see what his present was and then hardly even notice it? I walked down the hall and peeped into the study, where I witnessed a frantic husband wrapping a gift in the paper he'd just taken off his own gift. I chuckled. He may not be the most organized person in the world, but he surely is sweet!

John and I have spoken at the engaged couples' workshop at our church. One thing I encourage these couples to do is to share their thoughts about finances, sex, the role of parents, and so forth. Did John and I do this before we were married? Of course not! But what a world of difference there is now in understanding those differences in our background. And how much easier it is to enjoy each other with those simple tools.

When John was eight years old, his father was killed in an auto accident, so he grew up with a single parent. He learned early to be a saver, to cut coupons, always feeling as if he might not have enough.

I, on the other hand, lived on an estate with twenty-seven rooms—six bedrooms and bathrooms, four porches, four fireplaces—and my dad drove a Cadillac. Having money and new clothes was not popular at my school, and I hated being different. In my insecurity and desire to be accepted I'd walk the last two blocks to school so no one would see my dad's car. I'd deny it if someone accused me of having on a new dress. Money and possessions were not something I enjoyed. *Money wasn't so great,* I thought. Can you imagine the explosion when John and I got married? How many financial moments do you think we enjoyed? First I had to understand it. Now I laugh! John calls us a merger between Neiman-Marcus and K-mart!

Several years ago he came home on a weeknight and said, "Honey, get a babysitter. I'm going to take you out for dinner at your favorite restaurant." I don't mind telling you that I felt very special. On a weeknight, and at my favorite restaurant—one that John didn't even like.

I felt like a queen as we were seated and handed the menu. A few minutes later the waitress approached us for our order. "I'll have this," I said.

John looked at me and shook his head.

"What's the matter?" I asked.

"We're not having that," he replied. "We're having steak."

Well, now I was really elated. Not only was it my special night, but the expensive dinner as well! By now I was sure John had become Prince Charming, and my golden carriage was parked outside. "Well, all right then, I'll have this," I stated, pointing to the filet mignon. The waitress erased the first order, and John shook his head again.

Now you must understand that in all our married life my husband had never told me what to order. "What do you mean?" I asked.

John looked at me with eyes that said, "Carolyn, if you ever did what I said, this is the time to do it," but I was too flabbergasted to get the drift. The waitress was erasing again, wishing she'd never come to work.

"I don't understand, John. You brought me here and told me we were having steak. Why do you keep telling me no?"

"Because," he said, pointing to the bottom of the menu, "we're having this steak. I have a coupon."

Why didn't I see it coming? My lawyer husband has been late to court because he was clipping fast-food coupons.

One summer we stopped for breakfast on a trip to North Carolina. My mother was with us as well as our three children, Randy, Julianne, and Andrew. I know not to order orange juice in a restaurant because it's always expensive, but no one else pays attention to John's rules on juice, and everyone but me ordered "the forbidden fruit."

As the children began to drink their juice, they started complaining about the taste. My mother, who always tries to smooth things over, said, "Oh, no. It's fine. Just has a little pulp in it." Well, I tasted the juice and realized they had served us pure concentrate! Now what would a normal person do—call the waitress, explain the situation, and let her prepare the juice again? Not John—he just told her to bring pitchers of water. And we mixed and drank our money's worth in orange juice until it came out of our ears! Of course, nothing would do for my super-saver husband but that we drink every bit of it, and we stopped at every pit stop that day all the way to North Carolina.

I realize that sometimes laughing doesn't work. In my life, when it doesn't, most of the time it's because of my attitude. Our heart attitude shows up in all aspects of husband/wife relationships. Having fun together has a lot to do with how well we communicate. Being a good listener, really hearing what my husband says, is so important. John enjoys my company more when I listen sympathetically rather than try to solve his problems.

Good communicators also need to know how to talk. John knows I like the blow-by-blow scenario, while I have learned to edit my report for him. He wants it quick, concise, and in a nutshell. How many times have you seen men just tune women out when they get gabby?

One final thought: Don't get discouraged. These relationships are not all fun and games, but working on understanding the differences and learning to laugh at each other and ourselves really helps. Isaiah 28 reminds us that God builds us "precept upon precept, line upon line. Here a little, there a little." Life is a process.

I often remember a little song my son Andrew used to sing in kindergarten about God creating the sun, the stars, the earth, the moon, Jupiter, and Mars in just a week. It went on to say that God must be very loving and patient, because "He's still working on me." And wouldn't it be more fun, while He's doing the work, if it tickled just a little? ♥

Carolyn Jones is the author of *Who Am I, Really?* (Creation House) and has counseled for more than twenty-five years in the areas of emotional healing, marriage relationships, and adoption. She speaks at seminars, retreats, and churches, teaches Bible courses and studies at her local church, and has appeared on national television and radio programs. Carolyn is married to attorney John Edward Jones, who wrote *Reconciliation* (Bethany House), a book on healing relationships. They have three adopted children, two grandchildren, and live in Longwood, Florida.

Part Four

Deal With Problems

18

Through Tough Times

by Lindsay Roberts

W HEN TROUBLE HITS or tragedy strikes, I believe one of two things happens in a marriage. The husband and wife are either torn apart or pulled closer together.

Before Richard and I were married we both had experienced tragedies in our lives. He had suffered much pain from the world as a result of being the son of a famous evangelist, and he had experienced the deaths of his sister and brother-in-law in a plane crash as well as a host of other events that could have destroyed someone.

When I was twelve years old my father died of cancer. Many tragic events immediately followed, including much illness the next year. Then it was discovered my mother had cancer also. Miraculously, through medicine and prayer, God healed her. During this tough time my family realized we had a choice to split apart or pull closer together. Thank God, and thanks to my mother's great faith in God, our family drew closer together during our time of tragedy. It was a great learning experience to prepare me for what I would one day face in my marriage to Richard.

We were married in January 1980. At age eighteen I had been told I would probably never have a baby. After the first year and a half of marriage we began to wonder if this was indeed our destiny. We searched the Bible to find out exactly what it said concerning our situation. Then we focused on agreeing with the Word of God and with each other. There is great power in agreement. Matthew 18:19 says where any two on earth shall agree about anything, it shall be done by the Father in heaven.

After Richard and I stood on God's Word to conceive a child, we finally saw that dream came to pass. When I found out I was pregnant and that one of the desires of our hearts was coming true, I learned the hard way just how tenacious the devil really is. The first pregnancy resulted in a miscarriage along with surgery and other complications. The second also ended in miscarriage. Then, to make matters worse, the doctors discovered a tumor the size of a large orange in my right ovary, which seemed to be the only functioning ovary. He explained the risks of surgery, the possibility of a hysterectomy because of the size and location of the tumor, and the possibility of cancer.

This was the same kind of tumor my mother had had. My father had died of cancer.

Suddenly the reality of the devil was very evident in our lives. We were two people doing our best to serve God in, of all things, a healing ministry. Yet it seemed our own lives were falling apart. It didn't make sense except to note that when you are doing God's work you can prepare yourself for the fight of your life from Satan. He is against God's work and against God's workers!

A spark of hope lit when, during surgery, the doctors found that the tumor had disappeared. Several months later I discovered I was pregnant again. I cannot tell you the excitement I felt carrying a child full-term and going into a normal labor and delivery process. I delivered the most beautiful black-headed Cherokee Indian boy named Richard Oral. But the devil remained vigilant. Within thirty-six hours our precious son had experienced cardiac arrest four times and finally died. The shock and devastation we felt was indescribable. The doctors did their best to revive him, but all to no avail. Finally we just held onto him, believing that if we didn't let go, he wouldn't, but we had to face reality.

I wanted to run. I mean, I really wanted to run away. Yet I knew if I did I would never come back. It was the strangest, scariest emotion I've ever experienced. The one thing that saved me and our marriage was the unfailing Word of God.

Richard and I were both hurting. I ran to him for help and strength, but, unfortunately, he was as empty as I was.

We were both so devastated we couldn't lift each other up any longer. All we could do was hold each other and cry until there was no more tears and then cry some more. We made a conscious decision of our wills that we would pour ourselves into the Word and pray in our prayer language no matter how we felt. We decided by our choice, by our wills, that God was still God and that together we would let Him rule in our lives.

Richard had a trip scheduled to preach in Nigeria. He had all of his shots and papers in order. I didn't, because I had planned to be home with a new baby. His first thought was to cancel the crusade. After praying, we both felt that, since God had ordained the crusade and not canceled it, neither should we.

A friend had given me two tickets to go away with my mother while Richard went to Nigeria. I prayed and felt the leading of God to join Richard. Physically, it seemed crazy to go to a country like Nigeria just a couple of weeks after having a baby. But I sensed we needed to heal together. We needed to minister together. So Richard went on ahead while I got my shots and visa in order, and several days later I joined him in Lagos, Nigeria. That was the toughest ministry I've ever experienced because it was truly out of our need, our hurt, our pain.

Through all of this God asked me a difficult question: "Have I fallen off the throne because your son died, or am I still God to you?"

I said, "God, that's not a fair question!" I told God He was my God no matter what happened in my life.

He spoke back to me and said words I will never forget: "Then there's room for a miracle for you."

I knew what God meant. You see, in my pain and anguish, I had pointed my finger in Richard's face and cried, "Don't ever ask me to get pregnant again. I can't handle this." But deep inside I knew Richard hurt as much as I did. He didn't need my pain dumped on top of his as though it was all his fault. I repented from my heart and told Richard how sorry I was, but I wasn't ready to face another pregnancy. Not until God spoke those words to me: "Then there's room for a miracle for you."

To receive a miracle you must participate with your faith. Richard and I began to read all the same pregnancy, childbirth, family, Sarah-and-Abraham scriptures we had read before, and we got our faith and agreement back into action.

Six months later I found out I was pregnant with our Jordan Lindsay. She was full-term, delivered normally and a joy beyond measure. Two years later, along came Catherine Olivia, a beautiful, blue-eyed, blonde angel from God. Then, to add to the string of miracles, our sweet-spirited Chloe Elizabeth was born. God has honored our faith through tough times, and His Word is alive and powerful to anyone who will act on it! ♥

After her marriage to Richard Roberts, Lindsay began traveling with her husband ministering throughout the world, supporting him in whatever the Lord called him to do.

After the birth of their son, Richard Oral, "We were devastated when our son lived only 36 hours," Lindsay says. "But God picked us up, dried our tears, and helped us to try again. Jordan is our miracle baby. Through her birth, God has more than restored to us what the devil has stolen. Since then, God has added Catherine Olivia and Chloe Elisabeth to our list of miracles." Out of that experience, from pain to victory, Lindsay wrote the story *36 Hours With an Angel,* of how God sustained their faith and blessed them with the birth of their three daughters.

Lindsay Roberts ministers to hurting people alongside her healing evangelist-husband. In addition to cohosting Richard's daily television program, she speaks in churches and conferences through the nation and conducts her own Take Charge of Your Life women's conferences in Tulsa, Oklahoma.

19

In Control—and Hating It

by Lisa Bevere

THE YEAR WAS 1987, and I was stressed out, desperately attempting to be a professional employee, perfect mother, and wife. My firstborn son was not quite a year old. I was still nursing, which required pumping my milk at work and spending lunch hours at the caregiver's home. I was adamant that all his baby food be prepared with natural, organic fruits and vegetables, so I made it all.

My demanding work schedule even extended into my weekends. I faced both professional and personal challenges at the office. Through it all I tried to look and act perfect. I was careful not to let on that I was crumbling under the weight of the pressures and demands placed upon me. To accomplish this I maintained a rigid schedule, and I became obsessed with control.

Notice I did not mention my husband. There is a reason: I considered him to be the very lowest on my list of priorities. I justified my attitude by reasoning that he was an adult and could fend for himself. After all, these other areas demanded my attention and expertise.

Yet there was an even deeper reason for my lack of attention. John and I had learned to coexist in our separate worlds. When those worlds occasionally collided, they exploded with anger and careless words.

At that time I worked more hours than John and was solely responsible for the care of our child. I felt John was unresponsive and insensitive to my needs and the demands upon my life. I felt he did not carry his share. So I nagged, criticized, and belittled him in what appeared to be a futile attempt to change him.

John was not the man he is now. He was in a very uncomfortable time of transition, determined to find and fulfill God's purpose and design for his life. This pursuit consumed him to the neglect of all else. It seemed the more he strove to find God's direction, the more it eluded him. John became uncertain and unsure of himself. He hoped for this prospect or that, only to be disappointed.

I too was disappointed and discouraged. I was beginning to wonder if John could even hear from God. I was tired of working full time. I wanted to be home with my son, but I was afraid to quit. Frustrated, I had resigned myself to cynicism, developing an I'll-believe-it-when-I-see-it attitude.

When John would excitedly share with me what he believed God had shown him, I sighed and rolled my eyes. *Here we go again,* I thought. I became very quick and careless with my opinions. I was under the mistaken impression that God had put John and I together because I was so wise (in my own eyes, of course) and could counsel John. I saw it as my endless duty to share my critical wisdom and insight with him.

Often I was correct in my assessment, which I was quick to bring to John's attention. "See, I told you!" I gloated. I thought this revelation would cause John to realize the accuracy of my counsel and draw him closer to me. But it had just the opposite effect. I was a know-it-all who made John feel like a failure.

Sensing that his own wife did not believe in him, he pulled away from me. He took counsel outside our marriage. Both of us withdrew from each other.

I worked full time while John worked part time. He prayed for hours, fasted, talked to his friends, and played golf, while I was stressed and worried over insurance benefits and our financial provision. I resented his lack of involvement. I blamed him for all the pressure I felt. My employer was in the midst of a huge layoff, and I feared for my position. Worry and stress became a way of life for me.

Crisis Management

THE FACT IS we never actually faced a crisis. I was just planning ahead and worrying in advance for any future one. Soon my fears and anxieties overwhelmed me. I wanted John to feel some of the pressure I was experiencing.

But no matter how hard I tried to persuade John to worry with me, he would not. He declared that God had everything under control. I was certain God was not in control. In my eyes, I was holding things together, and I could feel my grip slipping. My response was to panic. I was convinced that John was in denial. "What if I lose my job?" I'd probe. "We will have no insurance benefits!"

"Are you about to lose your job?" John would ask.

"No! Of course not!" I countered. "But what if I did? Do you have a plan?"

"God will have one if that should happen," John answered calmly. "Lisa, just let go of this and surrender it to God."

Never! I would think. *If I'm not taking care of all this it won't get done.*

I felt so out of control that I tried to control everything that was within my power. I took it upon myself to remind John to do everything. I would nag him about the garbage only to find it sitting in the kitchen when I came home from work.

I felt it extremely important to remain responsible, and this meant worrying about everything. Since John was not willing to join me, I worried for the both of us. I was tormented because I measured our future and financial security by my limited ability to provide.

Sometimes my fears became so extreme and real, I'd wake John from a sound sleep to inform him that I was carrying much more than my fair share of stress. "If you would only pay attention to these things, I'd be able to rest," I complained. But he would not concede. He again suggested I give my heaviest cares to God and go to sleep. But I didn't want to give them to God. I wanted to give them to John!

On paper my reasoning sounds absurd, but it seemed very logical and sound at the time. My imagined fears were no less real to me than if they had actually happened. Some of you can laugh at me, while others may see yourself in my frantic panic.

Giving Up the Yoke

WORRY IS BOTH a noun and a verb. In its verb form it means "to harass, vex, irritate, plague and torment." I was definitely experiencing all of the above. I was tormented, so, in turn, I tormented. Worry is unbelief in action and it is fueled by fear.

I was constantly plagued by fear while worry choked the Word of God from my life. My mind was never at rest but constantly scrambling as I mentally ran the gauntlet of every imaginable crisis.

Needless to say, it had been a long time since I had known any type of rest or peace. Tension was my constant companion, and complaining and nagging my main form of communication. I was physically exhausted yet unable to rest. Even in my sleep I wrestled with my fear and worries.

I thought perhaps I just needed to wind down before I went to bed. So with visions of Calgon, I tried to relax by taking a bath or shower before I retired. In the tub I would submerge myself until only my nose remained above water. That way I could still breathe, but I did not have to see or hear anything. But even under water you cannot run from what is inside your mind. On other nights I'd shower until there was no hot water left, but to no avail. I still couldn't escape the internal and external pressures that weighed upon me.

Tension gripped my shoulders and neck like a taskmaster. I experienced the hopeless frustration of feeling responsible for something I did not have the authority to change. My load was too heavy because it was not mine to bear.

One night while in the shower I complained to God instead of to John about this heavy load. I whined and explained how overwhelmed I felt because I couldn't relinquish any of my burden to John. After all, if he didn't even remember the garbage, how could I trust him with anything more important? I wrestled back and forth, justifying why I could not relinquish control.

"Lisa, do you think John is a good leader?" the Lord gently asked me.

"No, I do not!" I asserted. "I don't trust him!"

"Lisa, you don't have to trust John," He replied. "You only have to trust Me. You don't think John is doing a very good job as the head of this home. You feel that you can do better. The tension and unrest you're experiencing is the weight and pressure of being the head of a household. It's a *yoke* to you, but a *mantle* to John. Lay it down, Lisa."

Immediately I saw it! The headship of our home was oppressive to me because it was not my position to fill. It would not be oppressive to John because God had anointed him as the head of the home. I recognized how I had jockeyed and fought for the lead position in our home. I realized how critical and faultfinding I had become. I had torn down my husband instead of building him up and believing in him. He, in turn, had relinquished his position of authority to me, and I had made a mess of it.

Broken, I turned off the shower and grabbed a towel. Immediately I found John in our bedroom. I wept and apologized for all my belittling and nagging, solemnly promising, "John, I will get behind you and support you. I believe in you."

I was not certain what I was supporting or believing in. I only knew John needed this support more than I needed all the details of what and why. I recognized that everything was terribly out of order in our home. I wanted God to order the chaos I had created. In turn John also apologized for not leading and for withdrawing from me. We struck a covenant to love, support, and draw from each other.

That night I thought I was dying to the hope of ever seeing my desires and needs provided for, but I did not care. For the first time in years I slept and found rest. My yoke of bondage had been removed.

Yokes and Mantles

TO UNDERSTAND WHAT had transpired it is important to know the meaning of *yoke*. A *yoke* symbolizes "oppression due to heavy responsibility, duty, or sin." It represents a burden so great you cannot escape it but are controlled by it. Its bearer has no authority over it; the yoke is the master. It signifies slavery or servitude. The phrase "to break a yoke" means to secure your freedom.

We are under a yoke of bondage any time we carry what God never intended for us to bear. This is not limited to marriage. Often as I minister I can discern when a person is under oppression, depression, and fear. Beyond the recognition of their outward effects, I can also sense the yoke's weight and strain on their shoulders. In the spirit I can see the person bent under a weight that is too heavy for him or her to carry. The person struggles and labors against it, but the yoke always oppresses him or her in the end. The yoke is not the person's to carry. This principle is not limited to natural marriage, but it includes anything we carry that we were not meant to carry.

On the other hand a *mantle* represents "protection, warmth, covering, and position." It was designed to be totally nonrestrictive, a sleeveless cloak worn over other garments. It was large enough to carry and conceal things within its folds. At night it was used as a bed covering.

A mantle's detail and ornamentation represented social standing or position. Samuel's mantle was fashioned by his mother as a miniature of the priestly garment. Joseph's mantle incorporated many colors, calling attention to him and exalting him above his brothers. Isaiah and John the Baptist wore mantles of animal skin, signifying their unique and similar prophetic callings.

A mantle covers our nakedness, conceals our faults, carries supplies, and announces our authority or position to those around us.

I had been yoked, and John had been dismantled. No wonder we were in a mess! When I submitted to God's established order for the household, my yoke was broken and John was cloaked in God's mantle of leadership. I was covered also, for the mantle spread to cover and protect me and all persons under John's care. When we are in proper submission to Christ, we are covered and cloaked in all that His mantle represents.

This principle applies to everyone—woman or man, married or single. Christ is your priest, protection and provision. Dare to trust Him and the authority structure He has established. He is our Husband and Advocate with the Father.

Construction Zone

AT FIRST IT WAS very difficult for me to relinquish control. But all the events of that last year had caused me to realize I had never really been in control—I had been fighting God's control.

As I surveyed the mess I had created, I knew I could no longer trust myself. It was time to let God's wisdom prevail. It was time to rebuild what had been torn asunder. (See Proverbs 14:1, NIV.)

By foolishly trying to build security and structure with my own hands I had inadvertently torn it down. I had demolished God's order. Unless God builds the house you labor in vain (Ps. 127:1). It was glaringly apparent that all my worry and stress had been wasteful and destructive to both my marriage and my health. Often when we are frustrated with the progress of God's process in our lives or in the lives of those around us, we decide to help out. But instead of building, we end up tearing down the walls of protection God provided for our relationships. This demolition occurs through the wrecking ball of criticism, belittling, nagging, and complaining.

In a desperate attempt to hold it all together I watched it slip from my hands. I grasped and clutched, only to open my arms and find them empty. I was so thankful that God had exposed my folly before it was too late.

So often we are afraid to trust God to build our home. So we take out our blueprints and start construction. When we run up against immovable walls, faulty foundations, and depleted resources, we cry out for help!

Perhaps you're at just such a place. God is waiting. He will step out of the shadows where He has patiently watched your frantic project. We have His gracious assurance that His plan is best. His blueprint includes meeting not only our needs, but even our deepest unspoken desires.

When I no longer felt responsible to affect changes in John, I could apply that same energy toward loving and enjoying him again. I was so thankful for God's mercy that I was quick to forgive what I perceived as shortcomings in John. I began to watch for the good, not the bad. Though none of our outward circumstances changed, the pressures were gone. I continued to work full time, but now it was different. I did not view myself as the source and John as the problem. I knew God was our source and the answer.

John was more settled and content. He no longer felt he had to earn my respect because I respected the position God had given him in our home. In turn he was more considerate. It was not unusual for John to straighten the house or have dinner ready when I got home from work. He even bought dishes and a washer and dryer as a surprise for me.

New Man

I WATCHED MY husband go from a boy to a man of the Spirit. There was a new boldness, decisiveness, and authority on his life. God answered every one of my prayers and exceeded my expectations. I respect my husband as a man of God, not just because I am commanded to honor and respect him, but because I believe with all my heart he is a man of God. I personally have experienced more peace, authority, protection, and anointing on my life since I relinquished control and threw aside my yoke. John is my best friend. He is my companion and a gift from God.

Where rampant confusion had reigned, faith, peace, and love now ruled. We were actually content. We enjoyed each other and the precious son God had given us. It was in this atmosphere that God's promotion for John came. There was no striving or struggling this time. When God's door opened it was clear and obvious. We were both amazed at how fast God set everything in order. God could trust us now because we were in agreement. The two were one.

Perhaps some of you have prayed for your husband to change. Release this burden to your Husband-Maker. It is too much for you to bear.

God's New Order

It is important to remember we are the family of God. He is our Father and we are His children. Before there ever was a church as we know it there was the family. God's plan for our households is better than ours — His provides protection, provision, peace and pleasure. It is a good plan because He is a good God.

We are witnessing this restoration in men. God is

turning their hearts back to Him. Because God is a Father, He is reminding them of their roles as husbands and fathers. When God leads He wants the men to follow. He wants them to be strong.

For too long women have been blamed for the weakness of men. The religious philosophy was: If the women will back down the men will be strong. The truth is that weak women don't make strong men. God makes strong men—and strong women. God never intended for women to restore their men. He will restore them. We must be in position to receive the blessing of this process.

God is preparing and commissioning men to lead their homes as priests, not lords. They will not be perfect priests. They will make mistakes. But are we willing to follow? God is preparing a priesthood to set His house in order. He is anointing them with hearts set apart to Him. This anointing will give men hearts for their families.

It is the answer to our prayers, but are we ready? Most likely God will not do this in the manner we expect or pray He will. For a season it may be uncomfortable and unfamiliar, but it will eventually bring refreshing and renewal. God will show Himself sovereign and receive all the glory. His plan will produce our heart's desire. ♥

Lisa Bevere is the author of the best-selling books, *Out of Control and Loving It!* and *The True Measure of a Woman.* Wife of popular author and speaker, John Bevere, Lisa is also a popular speaker in churches and women's conferences around the country. Lisa and John live in Orlando, Florida, with their four sons.

Material in this chapter was taken from *Out of Control and Loving It!* (Creation House).

20

When Opposites Attract

by Beverly Caruso

SUNLIGHT SPILLED INTO the bedroom, coating the bed with a brilliant glow. Rob turned on the shower, flipped on the stereo, and hummed along with his favorite musician. As Julie rolled over, she pressed the pillow against her ears. With a heavy sigh she finally peered from beneath the pillow at her bridegroom of two weeks. What's with this guy? How can he be so joyful, so awake at 7:00 A.M.?

Julie had been drawn to Rob by his exuberance and gregarious personality. Julie's family was composed of quiet, reserved parents and two sisters who, like herself, tended to slip gradually into each day. Is this the way all men are? Was Dad like this, and Mom toned him down?

This morning Julie again fought the urge to yell at Rob, to tell him to stop the racket, to sober up and act like an adult. So far she'd been able to control herself. But needing to exercise self-control while still half asleep was something she was unaccustomed to. *Am I going to have to live with this the rest of my life?*

My husband, Pete, and I teach marriage enrichment seminars. We often ask the couples to indicate whether one is a night person married to a morning person, whether one is a stay-at-home marred to a social butterfly, or whether one is an extrovert linked to an introvert. It seems universal: We seek and marry our opposite.

Sociologists explain that we seek to marry those who have characteristics we lack. God explains that we are intended to complete one another—"the two shall become one flesh." A marriage brings together two people who are to mutually contribute to and support one another in all areas of life.

Why, then, do those characteristics that first attracted us to one another later become sources of irritation and often painful conflict? One reason is that we each like to think of ourselves as being right. *My way is best,* we say to ourselves. For example, by nature I like to know where each dollar goes. Yet in our early years together, when Pete confidently purchased something "because we need it and I know God will take care of the cost," I was uncomfortable. Why? My way was what I understood. It was what I preferred, and still do.

Does your husband want to stay home after a day's work and you long to socialize? Perhaps you are the one who longs to stay home. Are you both intentionally trying to make the other miserable? It may seem that way, but the problem lies in two distinct personalities. Perhaps you are with people at work all day, yet because you are a gregarious person you still look forward to the stimulating fellowship of a group gathering. Your husband may work in a less public setting than you. However, if he is primarily an introvert he may be tired of being with people by evening. If you take time to explore your memories and feelings you might realize that each was attracted to the social nature of the other. Through discussion and loving compromise you may discover each one's needs and learn to meet them.

Sometimes simply acknowledging our inborn differences eases the internal pressure. More often we need to work consciously at the problem.

The first step toward handling our opposites is to choose to accept them. This means accepting my husband just the way he is. After many years of frustration with Pete's hard-to-get-the-day-started, late-to-end-the-day metabolism, I finally said to myself, *It's just fine with me that Pete is a night person and I'm not. I'll accept him and learn to fit in with him.* Now when I'm tired and he's sure he'll simply lie awake unable to wind down, I kiss him goodnight and go to sleep peacefully. No more begrudgingly lying in bed wishing to snuggle up next to him. I'm thankful there are plenty of times I feel like staying up with him.

Another important thing to do is explore the spiritual gifts God has given both of you. Has God given you the gift of mercy and your husband the gift of exhortation? If you study the various giftings in Romans 12 you'll soon realize that when you see a friend in need and want to rush to comfort him, your husband may be looking for ways to point out to your friend the weaknesses he believes caused the problem. You each are looking at your friend through a different pair of spiritual glasses. Step back and let God minister to your friend through each of you in His way.

Sometimes what seems to be an opposite characteristic is no more than a matter of degree. When Pete asks for a cup of tea, I know to let the water boil in the kettle. When he fixes me a cup, he pours it before the water reaches the boiling stage. Are Pete and I opposites in this area, or would someone else like her tea even less hot?

One couple I know uses a unique method to express their different preferences. When they were making plans to remodel their home, finding fulfillment for both seemed impossible. Finally the husband suggested they assign numbers to their desires. A ten meant intense feelings, a five indicated strong feelings, a one or two indicated only mild desires. By communicating the level of their feelings both husband and wife were able to get a sense of the other's views.

Areas of opposite characteristics in a marriage have great potential for friction. However, if we embrace those same opposites we can use them to keep the marriage vital and fresh. One of my friends, a bubbly woman, is married to a hard-working, pensive, and private man. Though he often prefers to stay home seven nights a week, he knows her interests in various causes provide fulfillment for her. He suspects they also help prevent the stagnation he's seen in marriages where the couple lives only unto themselves. He has become her "nodder," listening with apparent pride to her animated conversations and nodding in agreement.

Have you observed couples who have lived together many happy years? Often it seems they have become very much like one another—almost as though they started life together that way. They have simply learned to take advantage of their opposites. When we see in our spouse areas of strength we lack, we can look for ways to develop those characteristics in our own views. One translation of Proverbs 27:17 teaches that as "iron is made the finer by iron, [so] a man is refined by contact with his neighbor."

List the areas of opposite characteristics in your marriage. One couple I know found over two hundred traits where they either had once been or still were opposite. You and your husband probably have at least thirty ways.

Now mark those that no longer are a problem to your relationship. Discuss these with your husband, and fully enjoy those differences.

Then list in order of severity the remaining characteristics that cause friction in your marriage. Mark those in your husband that you know will never change short of God's intervention. Choose to accept these consciously, and commit that acceptance to God. Now use a different marking for those areas in your life that you need to change. Determine a strategy for overcoming them.

A word of caution is in order here. Don't become discouraged by trying to work on too many areas at once. Instead, choose one to work on and get started. Pray about each area daily, but ask God for special insight into your currently targeted area.

God said, "The two shall become one flesh" (Gen. 2:24). That isn't an empty statement. It's a commitment from God to work with us in the process of becoming one. As you allow Him, God will weave together your strengths with those of your husband. Learn to relax and enjoy the opposite characteristics in your marriage. Watch them add gusto to your relationship. ♥

Beverly Caruso has been a ministry wife for nearly forty years, over thirty of those in the pastorate. Her international ministry involves teaching and speaking as well as writing and counseling. She and her husband, Pete, have three children, and five grandchildren. Beverly has written five books including, *Developing Godly Character in Children,* (Joy Publishing), *Around the World* (Youth With a Mission Publishing), and *Loving Confrontation* (Bethany House). She serves on the board of advisors of Called Together Ministries, a support network for ministry wives.

21

My Brother's Middle Name Is Sandpaper

by Brenda Timberlake

Early in our marriage, I remember going to brush my teeth and finding that Mack had squeezed the toothpaste tube in the middle. His habit made me angry, and I verbally attacked him.

"Why did you squeeze the toothpaste in the middle like that?" I asked.

"That's the way I've been doing it all my life," Mack replied. Then we argued back and forth.

I said, "Well, then it's time for you to change. I don't like my toothpaste tube to be squeezed in the middle."

"When did it become your toothpaste?" Mack asked.

"When I married you."

"No, it didn't become *your* toothpaste. It's *our* toothpaste."

"Yes, but what's yours is mine."

"Let me ask you something. Could you get any toothpaste out of it?"

"No, I couldn't because you squeezed it in the middle."

"Let me show you how to squeeze it in the middle and get toothpaste out of it."

"No, I don't want it like that!"

I was too immature to overlook the fact that Mack squeezes the toothpaste tube differently. Another of Mack's habits I had trouble overlooking was his untidiness. I came home to find clothes strewn on the floor, making a path that eventually led me to Mack.

"Did you see you left some clothes on the floor?" I asked.

"I'm going to wear those again tomorrow so don't put them away," he responded.

"Then why don't you pick them up and put them in the drawer since you're gonna wear them tomorrow? I didn't marry a child; I married an adult! Didn't your mama teach you how to pick up after yourself?"

"Don't get my mama into this now!"

Mack's untidiness would aggravate me. I was thinking, *This is a grown man. He needs to pick up after himself.* And Mack was thinking, *If she would just give me a break, I would come back to get them.* (That's right; he'd come back the next day when he'd put them on.)

I was angry with Mack because I felt as if my rights were violated. Here I had spent time cleaning the room only to go back and find clothes on the floor. All my energy was wasted. I had a choice to allow this to bother me or to go behind him and pick them up.

A man feels the same way about his automobile. Maybe his wife drives his automobile and hits a mud puddle. Maybe she tries squeezing it into a parking space and the people in the car next to her open the door, leaving paint marks and dents on the car. He can choose to get angry, or he can say, "I'm just glad you didn't run into the side of a mountain."

Some things, such as bringing drugs into the house, should not be overlooked. But if a man drops his clothes on the floor, just pick them up.

Sometimes we get out of line with our relatives, friends, coworkers, church family, and even complete strangers. Unbridled anger is immaturity or selfishness on our part. If a person doesn't respond the way *we* want him to or do things *our* way, we let him have it with both barrels.

Learning how to deal with relatives regarding touchy issues can be challenging. Because we know each other's weaknesses as well as strengths, we will constantly argue unless one person is mature enough to overlook the other person's shortcomings.

It's important to learn to talk about what makes you angry and deal with it before the day is over (Eph. 4:26, NKJV). You may not be able to talk about it at the moment. But let your temper cool down— count to ten or fifty or one hundred—until you can speak in a soft voice. Be swift to hear, slow to speak and slow to anger (James 1:19, NKJV).

Learning to Count to Ten—or to One Hundred

YOU'VE HAD A long, hard day at work. As you're walking out the door your supervisor hollers, "Why didn't you finish that project? You've missed the last two deadlines! If you miss one more, you're fired!" Reluctantly, you turn around and stay late to finish the project. On your drive home you start honking the horn at the driver in front of you who is poking along. The driver doesn't know that you're angry because your supervisor made you stay late. After a one-hour trek, you come home to find the kids eating junk food before supper and fighting with each other. At the height of your frustration, you let them have it with both barrels. The kids go outside and vent their frustration by kicking the dog. Now everybody is in a bad mood—even the dog!—and the cycle continues the next day.

Many times we don't know how to harness anger's energy much less deal with it in a positive way. This unresolved anger becomes displaced anger. If Mack said something to upset me yesterday, and we've not resolved the issue, then when I wake up I'm still going to be thinking about it today. And I'll have another bad day. If we continue to ignore it, I'm still going to think about what he said days ago. This can go on for weeks, months, even years. People who don't let go of past hurts hold grudges over things that were said years ago.

Get a Tune-Up

DO YOU EVER wake up in the morning with your spiritual motor running rough, and you don't even know why? Maybe you had a bad dream the night before, and when you woke up, the first thing on your mind was how someone mistreated you on the job.

If you leave the house angry or in a bad mood you will carry that attitude throughout the day. Get a tune-up. Sometimes all it takes is one Bible verse to get back on course. Meditating on the Scriptures puts you in the right spirit. By meditating on the Scriptures, you begin to walk in the Holy Ghost, and He will guide you during those trying times.

Years ago when Mack would get really mad, the Holy Spirit would tell me to jump on his back and start tickling him—and I would.

I would tell Mack, "I'm sorry. Honey, whatever it is I did, I ask you to forgive me."

"You don't even know what it is?" Mack would reply.

"No. Tell me what I did to make you angry."

"First, you didn't cook what I asked you to cook. I told you to have . . . "

"OK, but you called and told me at five minutes to five, and I try to have your food ready by six."

"I don't know what it was you put on that plate, but it was lumped on there. What's the use of a man working if he can't even eat what he wants?"

"Honey, I asked you ahead of time what you wanted for next weekend, and you said, 'I never had a choice growing up, so I don't need a choice now.' I ask you to forgive me."

Then I'd start tickling him. Somebody in the household has to have the mind of Christ to keep peace. If you're a single parent, sometimes the kids can get on your nerves. But if you're walking in the

Holy Ghost, you have the power to walk in love. Ask for it!

Count to One Hundred; Then Don't Speak

AS LOVING AS Mack and I seem, we're still growing. We're constantly monitoring how we react and respond to our children. We have four children, one of whom is a teenager. Everybody knows that teenagers go through changes in life. Women and men in their thirties and forties go through changes, too. If you have teenagers and people in midlife crisis living under the same roof, you could have a real explosion. So somebody's got to have the mind of Christ!

If I get angry with Mack, I will go to him and say, "Honey, I'm sorry. I was tired, I was feeling bad, and I took my frustration out on you. Therefore, it's really my fault. I'm sorry I even said all those things to you. Please understand that I really didn't mean to say those things. I was talking out of fatigue."

Most of the time Mack is a lovely person. But there are those few times when he's not so lovely. I know not to even look at him. I'll leave him alone and say to myself, *Now, Brenda, he's been in the office all day counseling people aside from having to make one decision after another.* If your husband makes one decision after another, he may not be too pleasant when he comes home. Most men need a little break in between.

For instance, if I have been home all day without a soul to talk to, I may strike up a conversation with Mack as soon as he walks through the door. But if he's tired, he may not feel like talking.

I ask Mack, "So, Honey, how was your day? Anything happen today?"

"No, nothing! OK?" Mack says.

"Who did you see?"

"I didn't see anybody."

"OK. So nothing happened, and you didn't see anybody."

I know not to ask any more questions. I immediately try to have the mind of Christ and find out what I can do to help him relax. Normally a cool, tall glass of lemonade helps him relax. Or if I go over and say, "Honey, let me loosen your tie," or "Honey, can I take your shoes?" he loses his edge.

Learn to count to ten in dealing with displaced anger. In doing so, you become more sensitive to the voice of the Holy Ghost. As you minister to those around you, it will be only a matter of time before you see the power of gentleness operating in your life. ♥

Mack and Brenda Timberlake pastor Christian Faith Center, a 5,000-member, interracial church in Creedmoor, North Carolina. The Timberlakes are relationship specialists who minister in churches and conferences nationwide and on their weekly television show on TBN. Each month they also author *Charisma* magazine's popular column, *Living in the Real World*.

Material for this chapter was taken from *I'm Mad About You* by Mack and Brenda Timberlake (Creation House).

22

When He Doesn't Talk to You

by Laura Watson

W HY DON'T YOU ever talk to me?"

I'm sure I'm not the only wife to say *that* to her husband. But when it came to Brooks and me, we seemed to have no communication at all.

Exhausted from a day's work, my silent engineer would come into the house, plop in his chair with a book or paper—and we would spend the entire evening in virtual silence. I knew he needed a retreat from the rigors of the day. But I needed someone too. Scrubbing floors, washing dishes, cooking dinner, running errands, making up beds, and cleaning the bathtub are hard work also. And, unlike Brooks, who worked with people all day, I

161

worked alone. I needed someone to talk to.

On occasion he would sense my need, lay down his paper, and say, "What do you want me to talk about?" Invariably I would go blank—just sit there staring at him with eyes full of tears.

Brooks seemed content with the way things were. But I couldn't help but interpret "the way things were" as rejection. I branded him antisocial. And selfish.

He seemed to enjoy talking to people all day, but when it came to me he just clammed up.

It took a long time—and our own personal experiences with the Holy Spirit—before I began to understand. It wasn't until I listened to godly counsel from a small group in our church that I saw how much Brooks actually was communicating with me.

Week after week as the group met together for dinner, their first question would be: "Have you reached agreement about your house plans yet?" Their questions forced us to talk, to probe until we knew exactly what each other was thinking.

Our home group insisted we be together on house-related decisions before we began building. We were forced to communicate, to come into unity, because I wanted the house so badly. Here I was, an engineer/designer's wife, and for most of our forty-year marriage we'd lived in houses someone else had dreamed up.

The big problem: Brooks wanted an underground house. I wanted windows all around so I could see the beautiful trees out in the woods.

The group made me see that Brooks needed a challenge to motivate him into building his own home. When I accepted that as a "given" and agreed it would be OK with me, Brooks recognized my need for beautiful surroundings. He then told me I could buy some new furniture and decorate the house any way I wanted.

After this I began to notice other ways he is sensitive to my needs.

The house was almost finished. We were putting up florescent light fixtures one night when I slipped on the newly laid tile in the front hall and broke my arm.

Brooks panicked momentarily. Then he found a foot-long piece of leftover baseboard and two bright yellow Handi-Wipes. With these he fashioned a splint and a sling. Carefully pillowing my arm in the car, he drove to the hospital emergency room. The intern told us that was the best sling they'd ever had "come in from the field." But my awareness of Brooks's tender sensitivity was the best thing I'd ever had "come in from the field."

Another friend pointed out how polite Brooks is toward me, as well as to other people. He is a true gentlemen—pulling my chair out from the table, opening doors for me.

Brooks has always enjoyed bringing his friends into our home. Now that my attitude has changed, I can point with pride to the unique and beautiful home my husband has built.

Talking, I now realize, is actually an elementary kind of communication. God seldom speaks in an audible voice, yet He communicates. The greater language is the language of the heart. Communication experts say our words convey only about 20 percent of our meaning. More than 50 percent is conveyed by body language, and 85 percent by our attitude and spirit.

If our spirits don't have rapport, no words will get the message across. Brooks and I had to establish a basis for understanding: love and trust.

Brooks still doesn't talk much. We spend a lot of evenings working jigsaw puzzles in silence. But we are communicating—in the language of the heart. ♥

Laura Watson was an editor for Jamie Buckingham for over twenty years. She has been an editor and writer for newsletters, magazines, and books, including *A Christian Woman's Guide to Hospitality,* written with Quin Sherrer. Laura and her husband, Brooks, an engineer, have three children, eight grandchildren, and two great-grandchildren. The Watsons live in Palm Bay, Florida.

23

When He's Not a Christian

by Betty Malz

To LIVE WITH an unbeliever takes a special love. Ask God for that kind of love. Bless your husband. Make him happy. When he becomes happy, he will want to make everyone in the family happy too.

Pennie Langenback is very young, a recent bride. But her insight is wise beyond her years or experience. She said, "If he is unsaved and continues to resist, he will go to hell. So the only heaven he will ever know is the love and little bit of heaven you give him here."

Sara Douglas waited sixty-two years for her mate to come to Jesus. She once told me, "Don't talk to him about God, but talk to God about your husband. Self-righteous women talk too much. The Lord can do more with him in two months than you can do in two years. Silence and prayer make the best combination."

Most Christian women would not entertain the thought of being unfaithful. At the same time they may play a dangerous psychological game: bragging about Jesus. The unbeliever is spiritually blind and does not understand. He becomes jealous of another, better man—Jesus.

Janet was choir director, assistant organist, nursery worker, Sunday school teacher, took regular teacher training courses, was involved in Christian Women's Club, and met weekly with a ladies' prayer corps at her local church. Her husband threatened to buy her a cot so she could move into the church to save gasoline in running back and forth from home. Finally she realized she would have to wait for him to catch up so they could walk together.

How can two walk together except they agree? Most books and studies on spiritual growth are read by women. You may be one who needs to play it down, key it low, until he catches up.

There was a businesswoman we call Bertha Boomer in Baton Rouge. She married a French Catholic and immediately began nagging and coaching. The Sunday she finally got him to church, she jumped up during a joyous part of the service and started a Jericho march around the building. He was overwhelmed. "You started a religious riot," he said. To which she retorted, "You're spiritually blind," and rebuked the spirit of unbelief from him.

She turned him off before he got turned on.

When he did accept Jesus, he didn't tell her for

some time. "I've been a secret service agent for a long time. You're not God, Bertha. I don't have to tell you, to confess to you."

Do balance your witness with love. Pray for him. "I can do all things through [Christ] who strengthens me" (Phil. 4:13). Love your husband into the kingdom. When he sees you are real, he will want what you have. Your joy will be the undeniable sign of the presence of God.

Being born again does not solve every problem in a marriage, as you have seen in this book. It is merely the beginning of supernatural help.

Most people bring some psychological baggage into a marriage. By their fruit shall you know them, but by their roots shall you understand them. Pray for an understanding heart.

We spend from two to six hours a week in church—but what about the other 166 hours in the week? Are you pleasant to live with? If you are a success at church but not at home, you are a failure.

The Word is our hope while living with and loving the unbeliever. "For the unbelieving husband is sanctified by the believing wife.... For what knowest thou, O Wife, whether thou shalt save thy husband?" (1 Cor. 7:14, 16, KJV).

I have a writer friend, never before married, who married a widower with three small children. She thought she had died and gone to heaven. A month later she phoned me: "I think I have died and gone to hell. The kids don't want me to touch any of their mother's things, and silently my husband is comparing me to his deceased wife."

She called me again two years later. Her husband had quit going to church and had begun drinking.

She developed arthritis and was never free from pain in her spine and legs, and her fingers were in such bad shape she could use her word processor only with great effort.

One day she drove her car into the woods along a ridge road. She prayed, "God, make for me a way of escape if You will not save my husband."

The Lord spoke to her from His Word: "Bless them that curse you...be good to those who despitefully use you...love your enemies." Her husband had become her enemy, rarely defending her against the verbal abuse of the now "old enough to know better" children.

Every time he came home drunk she would pray silently, "Bless him, Lord." When he was gone she would pray aloud, "Bless him, Lord." When the children railed on her their hate, she would silently speak loving words to them with God's help. She asked God to help her love these live-in enemies.

Prayer and love broke through. In less than a year her husband had returned to the altar and rededicated his life to God. He has not had a drop to drink since. The children do not lavish their love on her as she had hoped, but they respect her and treat her as a close friend. To top it off, her arthritis is healed.

It works. Use the Word, pray the Word, and live the Word. His Word will not return void.

Ron and Vena Poole were divorced for ten years. Throughout those years Vena petitioned the Lord to send her husband back to her. Then she realized she was praying wrong. Her prayer changed to "Lord, draw him back to You." It happened. When he did return to her, he had been restored to being better than before. Today they have a counseling ministry for broken marriages and unequal yokes.

"Big Swede" was about as rough as they come. He was a lumberman, a harvest foreman who worked a crew of rough, hard-working lumberjacks in the north woods of Minnesota and across the border in Canada. His muscular 220-pound frame was hardened by exercise, but his heart was like a marshmallow where his wife, Flo, was concerned.

But all that changed when Big Swede started drinking. He became a vicious animal. For ten years he promised to quit drinking. For ten years she believed him.

I noticed on two occasions that Flo had changed her hairstyle. When I questioned her, she explained shamefully that it was to cover up the bald spot where Big Swede had pulled out large hunks of her hair on one of his wild drinking sprees. When he sobered up, he would threaten to kill the man who had done that to his Flo while he was drunk and couldn't defend her. He couldn't bring himself to believe that he and alcohol were the culprits.

To cope, Flo started drinking also. Along with her drinking came a passion for revenge.

One Friday evening Big Swede arrived home late. He was too drunk to eat dinner and fell across the bed fully clothed. Flo, drunken and full of spite, saw her chance to get even for ten years of brutal treatment.

Going to the woodpile, she found a long board with a large nail in the end. She returned to the bedroom, put a sheet over her drunken husband and knotted the four corners of the top sheet to the bottom sheet. Then, using a heavy thread, she literally sewed him to the bed by stitching the sheets all around. Only his head protruded.

All the hate of ten years surged through her as she picked up the board and beat her husband's body unmercifully—as he had beaten her. Blood oozed from the nail perforations in the sheet. She ran to the kitchen, returned with a box of iodized salt and poured it into the wounds of her moaning husband. Emerging from his drunken stupor, he flailed at the sheets, cursed, and threatened to kill her. She dropped the board and fled from the house.

She had already planned where to go. She hurried to the door of a "fanatic" Christian couple, begging for sanctuary until she could get a restraining order from the sheriff against Swede and file for divorce.

They prayed for her—and for Big Swede.

The second Sunday she lived with them, Flo agreed to attend the evening service at their church. At the close of his message the pastor said, "If you have a problem you can't solve, come kneel at this altar. God can fix anything if you give Him the broken pieces."

Kneeling at the altar, Flo sobbed out her confession to God, begging Him to forgive her and to protect her from her husband's wrath.

Rising to her feet, she was suddenly aware of the love of the people who had surrounded her at the altar, embracing her and weeping with her. She was also overwhelmed with an uncontrollable love for Swede. Was it possible, she wondered, for Swede to experience this love—and to give his life to Christ?

Two weeks later she returned home. She was simply trusting that Swede would welcome her back with understanding. If he came home drunk, would he try to kill her? A strange peace settled over her in answer to her solemn question.

She prepared a deep-dish peach cobbler for his homecoming. "Lord," she prayed, "as Swede eats each bite, let him feel my love and Yours for him."

The cobbler in the oven, she went into the bedroom. Stroking his pillow, she prayed, "Please, Lord, when he rests his head on this pillow, let him know the peace I know. Let him know Your love—and the new love I have for him."

Going into the living room, she sat in Swede's big brown recliner. "Jesus, when he sits in this chair, let him feel the rest You can give. Give him the strength to be the man he's really wanted to be these ten years."

Meanwhile, Swede was leaving the lumber camp. Inside he knew his drinking days were over. It was a strange, unexplainable feeling, but he knew he should go straight home.

His heart beat faster when he saw his old car parked in the drive. The smell of fresh peach cobbler filled the house.

Like a sleepwalker, he inched his way toward the kitchen. He saws Flo's yellow blouse bending over the oven—she was removing the cobbler. Tonight he was sober. He stood, trance-like, waiting—it seemed like hours.

Turning, Flo saw tears in his steely blue eyes. She had never seen her husband cry. He took his seat at the table quietly. He sat like a statue as she poured a cup of coffee into his earthtone mug.

Setting the coffee pot near the mug, she placed her hands on his head and pulled it against her breast, caressing his bushy head. She felt him shudder, then sob deeply.

Two weeks later, on a Sunday morning, Flo sat with Swede on the side of the bed and told him all that had happened to her. "I'd like to take you to the little church," she said.

"Naw," he said, almost shyly, "that don't sound like fun to me."

Throughout the service Flo prayed. Once again she knelt at the altar. "O God, do for Swede what You did for me."

Deep inside she heard a voice. "Your prayer is answered." She had never before heard the voice of God. She looked around.

There he was—all 220 pounds, prostrate across the wooden altar. He was weeping and trembling. "Please, God, give to me just whatcha gave to Flo."

Everything about him was changed. She had a new husband.

"Swede, what changed your mind? What brought you to that church?"

"I could stand that beatin' you gave me, Flo, but I couldn't withstand yer prayin'."

"But, Swede, you never heard me pray."

"No, I've never heard ya, but I *felt* ya."

Perhaps you're living with an unsaved husband. Want to really love him? Pray for him, as Flo prayed for Big Swede. Sooner or later he'll *feel* your prayers too. ♥

(Big Swede's story is condensed from an article titled "Big Swede" that Betty Malz wrote for the November 1982 issue of *Charisma*.)

Conclusion

by Betty Malz

Don't take yourself so seriously. My mother tells me I was born a seven-month preemie, wrinkled and skinny. Looking in the mirror this morning, it seemed to me I'm going out the same way. I think it's better to laugh at myself before others have a chance to laugh at me!

My husband, Carl, comes from a solemn family of educators. Mine is a family of clowns. On our fourth anniversary Carl's card to me read: "To the woman who taught me how to laugh." He has sanded some rough edges off me. We make a pretty good pair, but a sense of humor has helped to carry us through these eighteen years.

What is important for married bliss? It is not location, house size, clothes, money, or dining out—but determining to do the best with what you have. Be content and ask God to make up the difference. He will, but you must ask Him.

Here is something you can do to bring a focus to your own situation: Sit down and list the things you *do not* like about your husband. Next list the things you *do* like about him. You will probably be surprised when you compare the negative with the positive that you love him in many ways, that the good outweighs the bad. Then *throw away the negative list!*

Erma Bombeck wrote a column asking, "Where have all the good men gone?" Her answer was, "They are the homegrown boys, plain but quality, who are waiting for women to come down out of the clouds and say yes to them instead of yearning for what they can't and won't find."

Lowell and Connie Lundstrom were married at seventeen. They have had a long and successful ministry and marriage. He feels that many people wait too long, have too many choices, and become confused. Their philosophy: "You make him happy. He makes you happy. All the bases are covered. But when each person is in love with himself or herself— tragedy!" Commitment where you are now is vital.

All men are not created equal, but you can make what you have work for you. It is said that Eleanor Roosevelt never did win her husband's love, but she carved out a life for herself and campaigned for his success. Her tombstone bears this epitaph: "Behind tranquility always lies conquered unhappiness."

At a seminar I chatted with a most homely

couple. He told me, "We are the perfect 'ten.' While I was growing up I looked for the perfect ten. One day I realized I wasn't going to be able to catch a perfect ten. But I met a wonderful, perfect five. Five plus five equals ten. We are totally fulfilled and happy."

Here's an experiment: For the next thirty days let every day be Father's Day. Treat your husband like a king, even if he doesn't deserve it. Let him know what it could be like if he really tried, did his part. If after thirty days you don't see him become the person you are visualizing, relax a little, give it some more time, before you give it up to God. You are the pray-er; Jesus is the answerer.

The Scripture says, "In quietness and confidence shall be your strength...Rest in the Lord and wait patiently for him...Stand still and see the salvation of the Lord...Having done all, stand...Trust in the Lord, lean not unto thine own understanding, and he shall bring it to pass."

In marriage we are not individual tornadoes. We are a team, partners for a purpose. The Word declares, "One [shall] chase a thousand, and two [shall] put ten thousand to flight" (Deut. 32:30). Two lovers bound together with natural love plus God's love are ten times as effective as one alone. Many times unrest in a marriage should not be blamed on him or her, but on the enemy, Satan.

My stepdaughter, Carol, is married to an independent, self-sufficient man. He knows what he wants from life. Though he is self-contained, occasionally he admits to needing emotional support. Carol says the best way she can let him know he is loved is to support his decisions, which have proven through the years to be good ones. She allows him elbow room, space to develop, and respects his feelings.

Carol has learned that if she treats her husband with respect, he returns that respect to her. He shows an interest in her feelings and ambitions. The individualism of their marriage is not lost. Their nonverbal expressions, reflecting fairness and respect, say, "I love you!"

Everywhere I go people want to know how to get started writing. I tell them there's only one way to start, and that is to begin. It's the same way with marriage. Do you want to make your husband feel loved? Simple. Just do it. Love him. ♥

Other Books by Creation House

Couldn't We Just Kill 'em and Tell God They Died?

By Cathy Lechner

"Some family and friends you choose yourself," says author Cathy Lechner, "but others are simply thrust upon you.

Because you don't always get to choose who to love and when to love them, you sometimes feel like strangling some of them (well, maybe not quite!)."

With hilarious anecdotes, side-splitting stories, and candid insight, Cathy's book will minister hope and healing to your troubled relationships.

Out of Control and Loving It!

By Lisa Bevere

Lisa Bevere's life was a whirlwind of turmoil until she discovered that whenever she was in charge, things ended up in

a mess. *Out of Control and Loving It!* is the journey from fearful, frantic control to a haven of rest and peace under God's control. It shows how to surrender your life—your husband, children, finances, job, or ministry—to God. Are you holding on so tightly that God can't work in your life? Let go and discover the freedom and peace God intended you to have.